AFRICAN AMERICANS AND JUNGIAN PSYCHOLOGY

African Americans and Jungian Psychology: Leaving the Shadows explores the little-known racial relationship between the African diaspora and C. G. Jung's analytical psychology. In this unique book, Fanny Brewster explores the culture of Jungian psychology in America and its often-difficult relationship with race and racism.

Beginning with an examination of how Jungian psychology initially failed to engage African Americans, and continuing to the modern use of the Shadow in language and imagery, Brewster creates space for a much broader discussion regarding race and racism in America. Using Jung's own words, Brewster establishes a timeline of Jungian perspectives on African Americans from the past to the present. She explores the European roots of analytical psychology and its racial biases, as well as the impact this has on contemporary society. The book also expands our understanding of the negative impact of racism in American psychology, beginning a dialogue and proposing how we might change our thinking and behaviors to create a twenty-first-century Jungian psychology that recognizes an American multicultural psyche and a positive African American culture.

African Americans and Jungian Psychology: Leaving the Shadows explores the positive contributions of African culture to Jung's theories and will be essential reading for analytical psychologists, academics, and students of Jungian and post-Jungian studies, African American studies, and American studies.

Fanny Brewster, Ph.D., is a Jungian analyst in private practice in New York and Professor of Psychology at Pacifica Graduate Institute. She is a member of the Association of Black Psychologists and the Philadelphia Association of Jungian Analysts, and has been twice nominated for the Gradiva Award for her nonfiction writing.

"In this rich exploration of the psychological legacy of slavery and modern day racism, Fanny Brewster manages to hold to the value of Jung's ideas whilst also offering a serious critique of the racist roots of some of his concepts. In so doing she offers a crucial and potentially creative challenge to our Jungian community which largely persists in turning a blind eye to these matters and remains predominantly white. Whilst of considerable interest to anyone concerned with the psychology of racism, this book should be essential reading for all who consider themselves Jungians on both sides of the Atlantic."

—**Helen Morgan, Jungian analyst and Chair of the British Psychoanalytic Council**

"Fanny Brewster in her compelling book on *African Americans and Jungian Psychology*, makes visible what she calls a racial complex that has operated from the beginning birth pangs of Analytical Psychology with Carl Jung's own blindness to the current cultural context in his theory of archetypal psychology, to the silence of the Jungian community over the past nearly one hundred years to redress and address the blank spaces around race in the development of its theories and practices. The failure to include those forces that continues to generate the expressions of racial tensions and violence that appear daily in our newspaper and social media and the lives of many of our patients of color perpetuates another kind of invisibility. Fanny's narrative is a weaving of her fertile imagination in a way that opens Jung and analytical psychology's relationship to race and its cultural context of the presence of some of the same societal tensions that can be found haunting our analytical thinking and practices. She challenges the reader to locate him or herself in this current narrative so as to have an encounter with the other."

—**Samuel Kimbles, Jungian Analyst, San Francisco, US and author of**
Phantom Narratives: The Unseen Contributions of Culture to Psyche

"*African Americans and Jungian Psychology* is a revelatory, bold, courageous, and fascinating book that provides an examination and a critique of Jungian Psychology. The book champions the inclusion of Africa's contribution to the field of Jung Psychology, and for inclusion of people of color in treatment utilizing a Jungian psychological approach. *African Americans and Jungian Psychology* provides the reader with a powerful look into both historical, and contemporary views of Jungian Psychology and its relationship with African Americans. It is the first book of its kind providing insights never before explored."

—**Juwayriah J. Hassan, Certified Gestalt Psychotherapist, Staff Management Coach and Training Consultant**

"*African Americans and Jungian Psychology: Leaving the Shadows* brilliantly captures the essence of American Jungian Psychology and its relationship to African Americans. Fanny Brewster has written a ground-breaking book essential to our understanding of Jungian Psychology, and its influence on how we perceive and interact with one another in American society based on racial preconceptions. As we witness the beginning of new political and social movements in our country, this book is uncannily timely in its historical view of African American culture, racial complexes, and the psychological divide due to racial tensions in America."

—**Laura Wexler, author of** *Fire in a Canebrake: The Last Mass Lynching in America*

"This is an exceptional scholarly and penetrating analysis into the Eurocentric roots of Jungian psychoanalysis and the challenges that it faces in order to become more relevant in today's ethnic and racial divisive world, especially as it pertains to African Americans. Dr. Brewster observes how all of the Jungian complexes have been amplified by later theoreticians, with the one exception of the racial complex; this focused avoidance is what impedes Jungian psychology from any significant contribution to the American racial dilemma. This theoretical negation preempts the required knowledge and therefore empathy required and so beautifully explained by Dr. Brewster: 'When the African American client arrives for psychoanalysis this is the sorrow of generations that arrives with them- there is no way to leave it outside the door.' While this book is specifically illustrative of the challenges for the Jungian school of thought, I believe that it has much for all psychoanalysts to digest regardless of their analytic persuasion. I recommend this book for analysts who understand that issues of race and racism impact the analytic dyad, regardless of their racial composition."

—**Kirkland C. Vaughans, Ph.D., author of** *Psychology of Black Boys and Adolescents*

AFRICAN AMERICANS AND JUNGIAN PSYCHOLOGY

Leaving the Shadows

Fanny Brewster

LONDON AND NEW YORK

First published 2017
by Routledge
2 Park Square, Milton Park, Abingdon, Oxon OX14 4RN

and by Routledge
711 Third Avenue, New York, NY 10017

Routledge is an imprint of the Taylor & Francis Group, an Informa business

© 2017 F. Brewster

The right of F. Brewster to be identified as author of this work has been asserted by her in accordance with sections 77 and 78 of the Copyright, Designs and Patents Act 1988.

All rights reserved. No part of this book may be reprinted or reproduced or utilised in any form or by any electronic, mechanical, or other means, now known or hereafter invented, including photocopying and recording, or in any information storage or retrieval system, without permission in writing from the publishers.

Trademark notice: Product or corporate names may be trademarks or registered trademarks, and are used only for identification and explanation without intent to infringe.

British Library Cataloguing in Publication Data
A catalogue record for this book is available from the British Library

Library of Congress Cataloging in Publication Data
Names: Brewster, Fanny, author.
Title: African Americans and Jungian psychology: leaving the shadows / Fanny Brewster.
Description: Abingdon, Oxon; New York, NY: Routledge, 2017. | Includes bibliographical references.
Identifiers: LCCN 2016035101 | ISBN 9781138952720 (hbk.: alk. paper) | ISBN 9781138952768 (pbk.: alk. paper) | ISBN 9781315665351 (ebk.)
Subjects: | MESH: Jung, C. G. (Carl Gustav), 1875–1961. | Jungian Theory–history | African Americans–psychology | African Americans–ethnology | Racism–psychology | Psychoanalytic Interpretation | History, 20th Century | History, 21st Century | United States—ethnology
Classification: LCC RC451.5.N4 | NLM WM 11 AA1 | DDC 616.890089/96073–dc23
LC record available at https://lccn.loc.gov/2016035101

ISBN: 978-1-138-95272-0 (hbk)
ISBN: 978-1-138-95276-8 (pbk)
ISBN: 978-1-315-66535-1 (ebk)

Typeset in Bembo
by Deanta Global Publishing Services, Chennai, India

For my Parents Ruth and Robert
and the Ancestral Family who gave us Life

CONTENTS

Acknowledgments ix
Foreword by Polly Young-Eisendrath xii

   Introduction 1
1 Jung's early America: racial relations and racism 4
2 The reality of racial chains and the myth of freedom 12
3 American racial Black and White complexes 24
4 Africanist traditions and African American culture 31
5 African archetypal primordial: a map for Jungian psychology 49
6 Archetypal grief of African American women 63
7 The Jungian shadow 81
8 The dreamers of Saint Elizabeth Hospital 93

9	African American cultural consciousness and the Jungian collective	107
10	The promise of diversity	124
11	Summary: healing through an Africanist perspective	128
Index		*131*

ACKNOWLEDGMENTS

The possibility of this book began several years ago, even though at the time, I had no conscious intent to write such a book. It started when I was working on my dissertation, deeply involved in research on African philosophy and religion. A stirring occurred on an unconscious level as regards not only Africans, but also those of us of the African diaspora. This barely-felt stirring was an urge to write a book that actually acknowledged the relationship between African Americans and American psychology. The dissertation did manage to achieve this on a small scale, but I felt there was still something left unsaid, unwritten. Years later, I believe that *African Americans and Jungian Psychology: Leaving the Shadows* is the response to that initial call.

Many individuals, particularly teachers, have caringly supported me on my path as I grew into someone who could write this book.

I wish to thank my teachers—from kindergarten through my analytical training program—for sharing their love of story and language. They gave their time and talents, and this was for me the greatest generosity. The Harlem nuns who came to the segregated school in which I first attended kindergarten were my teachers for eight years.

Sr. Concepta, Sr. Francis, and Sr. Ann Marie have my utmost respect for teaching me the love of words. The power of their influence, and that of other nuns of the Franciscan Handmaids of the Most Pure Heart of Mary, provided me with an understanding of language when it had been, as a normal aspect of segregated Southern culture, denied my ancestors, as well as discouraged in my immediate family. I acknowledge the conscientious care with which they taught and instilled in me their love of words.

Janice Hassan has been a friend, a colleague, and a sister in spirit for close to 40 years. She has listened to my stories and poems and the frustrations and joys of being a writer. We have shared stories of our lives and those of our children.

When I spoke about writing this book, she was my stalwart supporter during all the early morning walks we took through Fort Greene Park. I thank her for this support through my writing years and specifically during the development of this book.

I could write this book because my teachers and fellow cohort students at Pacifica Graduate Institute allowed me to have the space and depth to think about and explore American Jungian psychology within an archetypal frame. Ginette Paris, Robert Romanyshyn, Lionel Corbett, Claire Douglas, Diane Skafte, Chris Peterson, Patrick Mahaffey, Avedis Panajian, Glen Slater, and James Hillman were teachers that have not only gently pushed me but have also carried me to deeply painful as well as joyful places as a student of psychology. Their stories and engagement with me has helped me build the courage to ask painful questions regarding theories and models of thought in which I could not immediately find myself, and required of me that I carve out a place in order to have a presence and a voice. I am grateful for their support in the development of my skills as a scholar. They provided me with the means to consider what our field of Jungian psychology required in this twenty-first century, and they helped me create a vision for how I might make a contribution.

The foundation of this book was created from the article "Wheel of Fire: The African American Dreamer and Cultural Consciousness," published in *The Jung Journal: Culture and Psyche* (2013). Chapter 8, "The Dreamers of Saint Elizabeth Hospital," was first published as the article "Wheel of Fire: The African American Dreamer and Cultural Consciousness" in *The Jung Journal: Culture and Psyche*, Volume 7, Number 1, pp. 70–87. Chapter 4, "Africanist Traditions and African American Culture," was first published as part of the dissertation *The Dreams of African American Women: A Heuristic Study of Dream Imagery* (2011), Ann Arbor, MI: Pro Quest UMI Dissertation Publishing. The poem "The Bridge" was first published in the literary journal, *Evening Street Review*, Number 13, Autumn 2015, p. 126.

The editorial support from Susan Calfee was crucial in shaping my paper into an article that would become the most important reference for the writing of *African Americans and Jungian Psychology: Leaving the Shadows*. Her encouragement and wise choices as an editor provided the preliminary structure for moving from article to book. Naomi Lowinsky, poetry editor of *Psychological Perspectives Journal*, gave me the opportunity to first publish several of the poems appearing in this book. I thank her for her generosity and kindness in allowing me to speak my word as a poet.

I have received consistent and valuable guidance from teachers, peers, and supervisors within the New York C. G. Jung Institute and Foundation community. Michael Vannoy Adams was the first peer in my analytical training community to reach out to me with acceptance, encouraging me to write a book that spoke to my experiences of multicultural issues in our Jungian community. Sylvia Perera is in the forefront of those who held my writer's hand during those years of analytical training. She read my initial writings, sharing her own gifts as a writer and offering me encouragement through the completion of this book. Phillip Zabrinski, Carol Zeitz, Jane Selinske, Janet Careswell, Gary Trosclair, Carolyn Sundstrom, and Linda Holahan were others who knowingly and unknowingly lent their support as I struggled to put words on the page. The rigor of my analytical training program was met with the rigorous compassion and support of these individuals at the New York C. G. Jung Institute and Foundation.

The teacher–mentors in my creative writing program at Goucher College guided me in building the consciousness I required as a writer to engage with the emotionally intense material of the book. Mentors Laura Wexler, Patsy Sims, Jacob Levenson, Diana Hume George, and Suzanne Lessard provided me with the necessary understanding of developing concepts and the craft for writing creative nonfiction. Their teaching has been invaluable.

Polly Young-Eisendrath has been a strong mentor support in my life as a writer. Her article from 1987, "The Absence of Black Americans as Jungian Analysts," provided a way for me to believe in my own ideas and ability to write about ethnicity in this area. She was writing from the perspective of an American Jungian analyst regarding race within the Jungian community when most others were silent, with the exception of Andrew Samuels in Europe. Without the support of Andrew Samuels, this book may never have been written. His own work in the combined area of politics and psychology has influenced Jungian thought for decades. His recognition of my book's subject matter and support of it helped me move my manuscript toward publication.

I greatly appreciate Susannah Frearson, my editor, who worked with me in reading and preparing my manuscript for publication with Routledge. I thank Rebecca Hogg, who also provided editorial assistance.

From the deepest place within my heart, I recognize and give honorable respect to my ancestors, my family, and my daughter Rachael, whose presence gave me the love I required to begin and complete this writing.

FOREWORD

Polly Young-Eisendrath

Many people are drawn to the psychology of C. G. Jung because it appears to be multicultural. More than Freud, or any other early psychoanalyst, Jung was interested in trying to meet those peoples and cultures (Africans, African-Americans, Native Americans, East Indians, and Chinese) that might seem to be the most exotically different from Europeans. After all, his work draws on archetypes which are defined as "primary imprints" on the human psyche—unconscious tendencies and dynamics that are universal. He contrasts these with "psychological complexes" that form in the emotional dynamics of an individual's development and early adaptation and continue to motivate unconscious thoughts, feelings, perceptions, and actions throughout the lifespan. Complexes are personal and archetypes are universal, and yet our unconscious complexes form around the core of archetypes.

To discover whether something is truly universal, we have to study and compare, as impartially as possible, different languages, cultural records, religions, symbols, dreams, styles, human gestures and facial expressions, and other forms of communication. We also have to take into account issues of equality and justice, because social, physical, and psychological oppression change the ways people see and express themselves, as well as the ways they are seen by others. Our own biases, prejudices, and stereotypes (conscious and unconscious) interfere with both our first impressions and our extensive interpretations.

As a student of Jung's psychology, I hoped that Jung's intention to be a "phenomenologist" and an objective "scientist" might mean he would be skeptical and careful about his own biases and interpretations of cultural and social assumptions and practices so wholly different from his own European, Germanic, and Greek heritage. Any careful reading of Volume 10 of Jung's Collected Works (1930/1968)—*Civilization in Transition*—will dash that hope. In my own training to be a Jungian analyst (I was certified in 1986), I was left feeling adrift and alarmed by a lot of what I read in Volume 10. Instead of being tentative or skeptical, Jung assumed that as a European psychoanalyst, he could know and understand people (because he understood the archetypes of the collective unconscious) who came from cultures and societies very different from his own.

I came to my Jungian training as a feminist, a Buddhist, and a White person from a working class background in Akron, Ohio, where Black children were among my best friends, and Black (then called "colored") families were ones in which I felt very welcome and at ease. Not only that, in the early 1970s I lived for four years in a Black community in North Carolina, where I was on the margins of the Black Power Movement while I worked for Upward Bound at a Black university (A & T State University, as it was known then) and my husband worked at a Black women's college, Bennett College. During that time, I felt privileged to be included in discussions of Black identity (albeit sometimes feeling very "White" among my friends and colleagues) and to come to understand the ways in which the Black Power Movement turned upside down most racist assumptions about African Americans. I witnessed personally how African American people learned to embrace themselves and their culture both in its historical African roots and customs (however much those were disintegrated through slavery and its legacies, they remained) and in the contemporary ways in which Black people created the beauty of art, music, dance, language, politics, and philosophy from their own suffering and oppression in America. They fashioned gold from the lead of their adversity.

My attraction to Jung's psychology in the late 1970s was propelled initially by having read his 1961 memoir *Memories, Dreams, Reflections*. Like so many others, I related to Jung as someone who had transformed his own messy and troubled childhood into gold—someone who had known anguish and even mental illness and had worked through those experiences to develop a comprehensive psychology of liberation (individuation) for adults. Initially, I did not know how much Jung was captured by the sensibility of "eugenics" (he was not a eugenicist, but he was taken by the idea that certain "races" embody different "levels" of abilities), which consumed many early psychologists at the turn of the twentieth century and left a destructive and delusional legacy of assumptions about "primitives" and hierarchies of IQ and human consciousness.

When I entered Jungian training in 1979 and witnessed the absence of African Americans in almost every setting (I eventually met Sam Kimbles) in which Jung's ideas were taught or discussed, I was uneasy and wondered what was wrong. Then, when I read and studied Volume 10, I could see what was wrong. I was distressed about Jung's unexamined assumptions of racial hierarchy and his stereotyping of minorities. I was more distressed hearing my Jungian colleagues speak about "the Shadow" being "black" and interpreting Black people in anyone's dreams as "Shadow figures," and assuming that the collective unconscious had a racial hierarchy built into it. When I said, for example, that Black people in my dreams were my friends and lovers, not my Shadow, my words typically fell on deaf ears. In place of a thoughtful critique of the naïve racist assumptions in Jung's writings, there was a kind of professional denial that anything was "wrong." Very often, I heard my elders say that Jung's ideas were "typical of his time and place." I thought, "That's true, but should we go on repeating his mistakes, now that we know better?"

In 1987, a year after I finished my analytic training, I published a paper titled "The Absence of Black Americans as Jungian Analysts." I wanted to open a discussion into the ways in which racism is a psychological complex organized in each individual around the archetype of Other or Opposite—and the splitting of Good and Bad—that leads to idealizing one kind of trait or person or family or group over against what is taken to be its "opposite." We all try unconsciously to find an "enemy" outside ourselves, onto which we can project what we disavow in ourselves. I also simply missed having African American colleagues. In the immediate years after that paper came out, nothing changed. Over time, though, thoughtful critiques and analyses emerged from Andrew Samuels (1993), Helen Morgan (2014, 2008), Samuel Kimbles (2014), Michael Vannoy Adams (1996), and Fanny Brewster (2013), among others.

And yet, there remained a gap. No major Jungian work examined both the weaknesses and strengths of a Jungian perspective for understanding and combatting the universal human problem of racism in groups, cultures, societies, and individuals. Still, from a larger cultural and social perspective, we do not have trustworthy models or methods for wrestling psychologically with the problems we have inherited from slavery and its transgenerational symptoms, or with the challenges raised by Black Lives Matter, or with our shared human tendency to find an "enemy" (to preserve the "good" in ourselves) outside ourselves. This volume fills that gap.

As an African American Jungian analyst, Dr. Fanny Brewster is knowledgeable and wise about both personal and professional experiences of racism and Eurocentrism in the Jungian and psychoanalytic worlds. She also knows the traditions of African healing methods and African religions, giving her a broad perspective on symbolism and clinical work. She writes from personal experience and she writes from the experience of addressing issues of race and Otherness inside the consulting room, in supervision, in training sessions and conferences, and in both American and non-American (especially European) Jungian thought. What is especially impressive in this book is that Brewster reviews the vast literature on Africanist healing cultures and Jungian healing archetypes with an eye to finding what can be helpful to (1) waking us up to our racism (because it largely comes from unconscious assumptions and perspectives), (2) communicating with each other as psychoanalysts and mental health professionals about how racism functions in treatment and supervision (even if the two people share the same skin color), and (3) applying Jung's psychology, with its emphasis on archetypes and complexes and the projection of Otherness, to provide a way of becoming aware of the legacies of racism, slavery, oppression, and their transgenerational symptoms in our clinical work.

Brewster wants Jungians in particular, and psychoanalysts in general, to stop exempting themselves from recognizing and understanding the roots of their own racism. She wants us to "grow up" and move beyond idealizing our founders and ancestors, feeling that we cannot differentiate from a kind of defensiveness that still exists about our originators' ideas. She wants us to see that envy and hatred are natural aspects of the aggression of early life for all humans, and then to see how these aspects can be "assigned" to those who seem to be Other, especially people of color, who may have origins different from our own. Whatever our skin color, we must understand that "race" is not a reality but a categorization of people as "Whites" and "Negroes" invented by slave owners to protect themselves and their wealth and to oppress others. As writer and journalist Ta-Nehisi Coates observes in his 2015 memoir *Between the World and Me*, about being Black: "Black" people are bound not by a biological "race" or any uniform skin color. Instead, they are bound by the ways they have suffered and "by all the beautiful things, all the language and mannerisms, all the food and music, all the literature and philosophy, all the common language that they have fashioned like diamonds" (119).

Using any analysis of "race" or "racial differences" at this point in time is an egregious mistake because it is based on a delusional idea—the idea that difference in skin color or facial features translates into some kind of inherent mental or psychological difference. Instead, racism is a defensive projection of something we cannot see or tolerate in ourselves. Brewster gives us all kinds of examples of how we all, no matter our skin color, project our own disavowed sexual, hateful, and aggressive tendencies into those who are vulnerable or appear to be Other. This is a root cause of humans oppressing one another. No psychoanalytic theory or idea should ever provide any justification for hierarchies of human consciousness or intelligence based on the false category of "race." Instead, we psychoanalysts should invite people to see into and analyze their own racist complexes and desires.

Brewster invites us to imagine that we are on the horizon of a new kind of consciousness—one that might allow us to heal collectively from a traumatic past in which surplus wealth came from slavery and oppression and served only those people who controlled power and resources. That past continues now as violence against people of color, as forced labor in prisons, and as racial profiling. How can we use the paradigm of Jungian archetypes and complexes to unpack our collective and individual racist complexes and personal prejudices? We have to begin in our own psychoanalytic backyard and revise our concepts and assumptions, and then extend that process outward. Ever since I grew up in Akron, Ohio, in racially mixed schools and churches, I have hoped for the possibility of healing the pain of racism. Brewster's invitation here to "leave the shadows"—and bring out into the open the whole range of possibility and trauma, of unconsciousness and awakening, and of inquiry and conversation—has given me hope that we might be approaching a new horizon of human consciousness.

References

Coates, Ta-Nehisi (2015). *Between the World and Me*. New York: Little Brown.
Jung, C. G. (1993). *Memories, Dreams, Reflections* (13th ed.). New York: Random House.

INTRODUCTION

> Between me and the other world there is ever an unasked question: unasked by some through feelings of delicacy; by others through the difficulty of rightly framing it. All, nevertheless, flutter round it. They approach me in a half-hesitant sort of way, eye me curiously or compassionately, and then, instead of saying directly, How does it feel to be a problem? They say, I know an excellent colored man in my town; or I fought at Mechanicsville; or Do not these Southern outrages make your blood boil? At these I smile, or am interested, or reduce the boiling to a simmer, as the occasion may require. To the real question, How does it feel to be a problem? I answer seldom a word.
>
> W. E. B. Du Bois, *The Souls of Black Folk*

The problem of racism in America is complicated, while the central idea of race itself is simple. We are one race with centuries-old constructs and ideas regarding what potentially makes us enemies of one another, due only to ethnological differences.

African Americans have been at the psychological suffering end of America's racial *problem* for centuries. This began with slavery and has continued through until the current time. The psychological effects of prejudice and racial hatred, embedded in every aspect of American life, have been a profoundly painful experience, in every way imaginable, for African Americans.

We continue to live in a social reality where African Americans are considered a problem—if not *the* problem—by other Americans of varying ethnic groups. At the time of this writing, nearing the end of the presidency of the first African American in our history, racial issues and conflicts dominate our media and social dialogues.

The tenor of our society and its institutions, despite laws to create equality and change, continues with an undercurrent of belief that African Americans *are*

America's problem. Racism is not viewed as the problem, only our skin color, simply *because* of our skin color.

African Americans and Jungian Psychology: Leaving the Shadows focuses on a broad and yet deep-running aspect of African American life—our culture, and our psychology as one aspect of this culture. This writing not only seeks to explore how African Americans exist as a cultural group with a particular cultural consciousness; it is also an attempt to go further, investigating C. G. Jung's Analytical psychology, or Jungian psychology as it is better known, looking at its development into an American Jungian psychology with racism as a lingering main characteristic. It is crucially important to explore and deepen our understanding of the historical racial relationship of Jungian psychology to African Americans. This relationship begins with Jung's own exploration and confiscation of African cultural principles and ideologies in the first half of the twentieth century. Jung was able to use African ideologies, indicating the importance of the need for them with Europe's deprived "modern man," while being disparaging of the African—the *primitive* and *savage*, from whom he *took* the ideas.

In my discussion of Jungian psychology and racism, I wish to explore the conscious, and perhaps unconscious, motivations against an integrative model of Jungian psychology that could possibly exist in service to African Americans.

Many more African Americans seek psychological services than ever before. Yet, the number of those who enter Jungian psychology for clinical work, or to be trained as analysts, continues to be exceedingly low. I discuss this as a reflection of the larger issue of American racism in the field of psychology and in American society.

I specifically discuss racism as the inherent problem of a racial divide that has existed since Jungian psychology first came to America as a psychoanalytical practice in the early 1900s. Racism was built into American Jungian psychology regardless of it having European roots.

There continues to be a quiet turning away or absolute silence by many of those practicing within the area of American Jungian psychology as regards racist language and theoretical concepts in Jung's writings and speeches. The irony of this situation is that much of Jungian psychology was built on the basis of an Africanist cultural foundation that Jung termed *primitive*.

Who was C. G. Jung in terms of his thinking as regards African Americans? What is available to African Americans through the act of re-claiming and re-collecting the African cultural attributes and ideas that were used by Jung to establish his form of psychoanalytical psychology? During the time of American slavery, many individuals worked to save the lives of African Americans through the Underground Railroad. Leaving a light in the home window was a signal that it was safe for slaves to approach the house on their escape from plantations. The house offered shelter on the passage from Southern slavery to Northern freedom.

It is my hope that *African Americans and Jungian Psychology: Leaving the Shadows* will provide us with better sight for seeing into the shadowy darkness of an apparent still-present racism. It might perhaps give us a new place of consciousness in which to move as we deepen the practice of American Jungian psychology, making it available for all by the elimination of that which keeps it in the shadow of racism.

# 1

JUNG'S EARLY AMERICA

Racial relations and racism

American Jungian psychology as practiced, and related to African Americans, has barely changed since its inception by Jung 100 years ago. The Eurocentric focus of Jungian psychology, without consideration of a positive Africanist cultural context, continues to hold on to its European roots, which remains alienating to many African Americans. This is largely due to Jung's own early writings from the *Collected Works*, his interviews during time spent on his few visits to America, and his autobiography, *Memories, Dreams, Reflections*. American Jungians in the practice of Jung's psychology continue, with few exceptions, to teach and train individuals to become analysts with little acknowledgment of current American antagonistic racial lives or the necessity of a cultural context within the American Jungian analytical frame. It almost appears as an unspoken code that if this cultural context continues to be ignored, it will disappear. This is one of the main features of American racism—making and treating African Americans as if we are invisible, as if we do not exist, except to be of service.

Jung initially identified African Americans within his collective unconscious theory as being and carrying *the Shadow*—his principal archetype for all that was negative within the unconscious. The theoretical idea of shadow and the Shadow archetype have grown and been expanded upon in recent writings by some Jungians within the last two decades. Jung's concept of the Shadow was initially discussed by him in the following manner:

> Closer examination of the dark characteristics—that is, the inferiorities constituting the shadow—reveals that they have an emotional nature, a kind of autonomy, and accordingly an obsessive or, better, passive quality. Affects occur usually where adaptation is weakest, and at the same time they reveal the reason for its weakness, namely a certain degree of inferiority and the existence of a lower level of personality. On this lower level with its

uncontrolled or scarcely controlled emotions one behaves more or less like a primitive, who is not only the passive victim of his affects but also singularly incapable of moral judgment.

(CW 9, part II, Para. 15)

From this early development of Jung's concept of shadow, subsequent Jungian analysts developed a general idea used in reference to people of color. This most specifically occurred in Jungian dreamwork. Jung's words above can be compared with those of Marie-Louise von Franz and Fraser Boa in *The Way of the Dream: Conversations on Jungian Dream Interpretation* (1994: 107); in speaking with a White dreamer who shares with von Franz about one of his dreams, she gives this response:

> The black garment represents a typical feature of the undeveloped inner anima figure. Just as we shall see that the animus in women is sometimes destructive and negative, the black anima is relatively negative in a man. The black anima indicates that his whole capacity to love is mostly autoerotic…. The peeling of the skin of the black female and the transformation into a white golden anima is the transformation of the loving capacities of a man, the transformation of his Eros from a *primitive autoerotic fantasy into a true human capacity*.
>
> (Author italics)

Unfortunately, the image of African Americans in Jungian dreamwork as shadow, or the Shadow, was a major component of the work for decades. In changing times, the definition *shadow* was used to include not only the negative qualities of the unconscious but also a psychic location where we store all types of personal material that it is emotionally difficult to accept. This material may be considered by the ego to be positive or negative. However, the initial Jungian understanding of shadow was that it was negative, dark, and primitive and belonged to that of the primitive.

However, within the major teaching institutes, public programs, and literary training tools of American Jungian psychology—the *Collected Works*—the racial, non-multicultural thinking of Jung's psychology continues to survive without any disclaimers or updating.

Jung, a protégé and later colleague of Freud, was present in the beginning days of psychoanalysis. After his separation from Freud in 1912, Jung began the development of his own type of psychoanalysis, which he called *analytical psychology*.

Jung began his career at Burgholzli Hospital in Switzerland as a medical doctor working with schizophrenic patients. He became interested in how they fantasized, their dreams and delusions. In his private practice, Jung noticed that there were similarities between patients in both settings. This eventually led him to explore historical teachings regarding *archetypes*, or what he also later called the *collective unconscious*.

Jungian psychology is but one part of the broader field of American psychology. The establishment of Jungian psychology began in the early days of the twentieth century. Jung saw an opportunity for the creation of his particular type of psychoanalysis as opposed to that of Freud, who did not have the same level of interest as Jung in bringing psychoanalysis to America.

Freud said, after his first and only visit, that "America was a mistake." The context within which he made this statement implied that there was little merit in attempting to bring his psychoanalysis to America. It was a country unworthy of it. Jung may have felt that he could become a pioneer in the more open field that America presented since Freud was already established in Europe.

Jung's early relationships were with men such as G. Stanley Hall, William Alanson White, and Trigant Burrow. Though he had initially come to America with Freud, Jung later made trips unaccompanied by him. As their friendship deteriorated and Jung began to experience the emotional loss of his closeness with Freud, America might have been a way to become more of his own person in being identified with the *new* psychoanalysis—analytical psychology.

When Jung arrived in America in 1912, his main purpose was to engage in activities that would support his collective unconscious thesis: that race was not a factor in the archetypal realm—in the collective unconscious. He believed that he could confirm this idea by "testing" African Americans. Jung had already been exposed minimally to members of this ethnic group on his previous two trips to America. It was his belief that a study with this group would solidify a major point of his argument regarding archetypes.

Jung journeyed to Baltimore where he visited with Burrow. From there, he proceeded to Washington, D.C., where he remained for a month, interviewing and collecting the dreams of several African American men residing at the St. Elizabeth Hospital. Jung states in his *Collected Works* that one of the dreamers had a dream of Xion. Jung surmised that the dreamer could not have known about the Greek myth, nor about the symbolic wheel of the dream, and that therefore the dreamer had had an archetypal dream. He felt that this proved his point that the archetypes of the collective unconscious were not racially inspired energies.

As far as Jung has stated regarding this experience with the dreamers, he did not collect nor was he interested in the related *cultural* or *associative psychological* material from the dreamers. During the time that Jung completed his "study" on these dreamers, it would not have been unusual for patient information to have been collected and used for the purpose of the medical staff without the permission of family or outside governmental authority. This has only been a factor in more recent times with society's recognition of the need for patient's rights and privacy and their advocacy of these rights.

The idea of the collective unconscious was a very important one that Jung was eager to claim as a part of his own theoretical base and as a distinguishing mark to separate him from Freud. In his research, Jung wished to prove that the unconscious was not bound by race. He wanted to show *empirical studies* that everyone, regardless of *racial identity*, belonged to the collective unconscious. Not only were archetypes in the imaginal life of schizophrenic patients, they were also present in his normally neurotic patients.

To prove the existence of archetypes across racial boundaries, Jung decided to come to America and do this research *on* African Americans. I say *on*, rather than *with*, because in those early days of experimental research and studies, patients were most times not given options for consent to treatment. Families frequently left mentally ill or physically disabled members in the care of hospitals and doctors who had broad rights of treatment without family interest or consent. This is the type of setting that Jung entered to conduct his empirical study of African Americans in 1912. Thanks to the help of William Alanson White, then chief administrator of St. Elizabeth Hospital in Washington, D.C., Jung was given full access to 15 African American male patients. Jung reports that he recorded their dreams for a month during the time he stayed at the hospital.

As a result of his research with this group of African American men, Jung claimed that his hypothesis regarding the nonracial nature of the collective unconscious was correct. The men of Jung's study were not named or recognized in any way by Jung other than as his subjects. This manner of treatment by Jung, though not unusual within medical and all other societal circles, underlies one of the still-present problems affecting American Jungian psychology in its relationship with African Americans.

Jung was not so different in his way of treating these African American men than was racially customary in 1912 America. His behavior actually fit well into American society's generally racist treatment of African Americans during those times. In this way, Jung is a "man of his times," as is frequently said by Jungians in justification of Jung's negative cultural attitude and comments regarding African Americans.

African Americans in these days of the introduction of psychoanalysis to America were attempting to survive in a post–Reconstruction Era that saw the rise of racism in the form of the Ku Klux Klan (KKK). In the first two decades of the twentieth century, African Americans were still traumatized by White race riots and lynching. The 1921 Tulsa, Oklahoma, race riot by Whites resulted in the killing of up to 300 African Americans and the destruction of the entire community of Greenwood. In Florida in 1923, the African American town of Rosewood was completely destroyed by rioting Whites. In both of these instances, the given cause for White aggression was the attack and rape of White women by African American men. These are only two examples of the violent hatred expressed by White Americans in the years when psychoanalysis was just being established in America.

There is no mention in American Jungian psychology literature of the impact or influence of White racial violence, African American slavery and its effects, or the significance of race within psychoanalytical work—with the very limited exception by Jung. These exceptions were generally of a negative reflection on African Americans and are noted through various chapters within this book. Jung's recognition and *acceptance* of the KKK as only a social group attempting to regain some primal experience of brotherhood, like the Knights of Columbus, was very far from the American political truth as any African American knew. Jung did not offer any possible solace through the psychology he was beginning to establish in America. In fact, he indicated that Jungian psychology was actually not for anyone of African ancestry.

The atmosphere of what appears to be "permitted" violence against African Americans continues until today. During 2014, African American males died at the hands of law enforcement officers in areas as far reaching as New York City to Ferguson, Missouri. The deaths of Michael Brown, a teenager killed in Ferguson; Trayvon Martin, killed by George Zimmerman in Florida; and Eric Garner of Staten Island, New York, have galvanized Americans from different ethnic groups in support of changing the politics and racial aggression of law enforcement agencies. Police seem to be or feel empowered to kill at will, based on their inappropriate use of gun power and military-like force. A recent question raised in this current state of social upheaval regards the acceptability of local police officers being armed with warlike weapons. Are such heavy guns, armor, and military tanks necessary or desirable against America's citizens?

On August 14, 2014, the *USA Today* newspaper reported the following:

> On average there were 96 cases of a white police officer killing a black person each year between 2006 and 2012, based on justifiable homicides reported to the FBI by local police … the FBI's justifiable homicides database paints only a partial picture—accounting for cases in which an officer killed a felon. It does not necessarily include cases involving victims like Michael Brown, Eric Garner, and others who were unarmed when confronted by police.

Since this is the political climate of America's social scene, demonstrations have taken place in cities and towns all over America. How do we engage with the thinking and feeling aspects of individuals within these communities? What is life like psychologically for African Americans, who continue to be faced with issues of racism in what purports to be a multicultural society with equal justice before the law? We are in fact a multicultural society, but we are not one in spirit. Racism impedes this possibility.

The issues of racism in Jungian psychology stem from when psychoanalysis began to take hold in America. At that time and long since, there has been little one could say that has made psychoanalytic work appealing to African Americans, though this has not been consistently true for the Freudian psychoanalytical community. The stigma of being considered strange, different, *primitive*, or Other—the language of Jungian psychology, infused with the possibility of racism—greatly decreases psychological options for African Americans in the area of Jungian psychology. There may be an absence of analytical sessions between the White analyst and African American patients due to the nature of American racial relations.

This is a feature within the field of American psychology, but it is particularly relevant from the perspective of Jungian psychology. Of course, African Americans are more likely now than ever before to seek out psychological help, but I believe a racial stigma relating to Jungian psychoanalysis remains.

The number of African American psychotherapists graduating from colleges who can be available to African American clients has certainly increased since the turn of the twentieth century, when there were none; however, the number of individuals of color who choose to seek out Jungian-oriented psychological help remains comparatively small. In addition, the number of African Americans who choose to become Jungian analysts continues to be exceedingly small. What could be the reasons for such a situation?

How much of the trauma from society's racial bent continues to haunt potential non-White Jungian patients and those wishing to become analytical psychotherapists based on Jung's early theoretical model?

Is the nature of psychoanalysis off-putting to African Americans because of its insistence on the individual rather than family, or is it the distance of being "analyzed" rather than intimacy of a known healer? The African American experience, drawn psychically from Africanist consciousness, holds that the family group is important.

There is a place of reverence for those who have come before, and they are still present in contemporary life through prayers, memories, and dreams. Words, and the understanding of a mutually understood language, matter to a great degree. The following quote is by Thomas Parham and Joseph L. White from their book, *The Psychology of Blacks: An African American Perspective*:

> In the theoretical model of Black psychology presented by Wade Nobles (1976), interrelatedness, connectedness, and interdependence are viewed as the unifying philosophic concepts in the Afro-American experience base. The concepts are prominent themes in Black language with respect to the interactive dynamics between speaker and listener, the power of words to control, cognitive style, timing, and communicative competence.... Through the spoken word linkages are established across time and space, transmitting the Afro-American heritage from one generation to another.
> *(Parham and White, 1990, p. 63)*

Most significant is the issue of identity amongst African Americans.

American psychology developed from a model of 1:1 and has eventually moved in the direction of acknowledging families and significant others. This is a model that would appeal to African Americans since the African worldview is not only that of the individual but also that of the group, the tribe, the village. Group therapy has made gains in America's psychology profession but not within the psychoanalytical model.

As psychological training institutions have grown in America, they have attempted to adopt the idea of the cohort—learning and traveling through "life" at the institute with your "tribe." This doesn't always translate in the analytical space where therapist and patient sit opposite one another trying to find warmth and intimacy in the therapeutic alliance. In my own experiences with African American analysands, there is an expectancy of closeness and interconnectedness that goes far beyond that of White analysands. The idea of limits in the relationship when patients are suffering emotionally does not exist. They want to know that I am hearing and being *fully* present for their emotional pain. This is indicated at times not only by my voice but also by my physical presence, a sense of being more in touch with theirs in the phenomenological field. Anything other than this looks like rejection and shaming in their moment of exposure and vulnerability. The training of an analyst is to be completely present with the patient. How this can be achieved in those moments of analytical work can be very different based on the ethnicity of analyst and patient.

Cultural differences are a factor in American life, a life that includes American psychology as a field where we go to get relief from trauma and hope for healing. A few books have been written reviewing the differences that occur between a psychotherapist and his or her patient because of their ethnicity, but this is rare in the Jungian literature. In part, this could be because there are so few African American Jungian analysts to write about their patient's clinical experiences. It might also be because the number of African American clients who receive analytical psychoanalysis is very limited.

America says that it is a country that welcomes and believes in multiculturalism. This is the collective word given at a time when gays, women, and some ethnic groups are gaining more political power in the society. Within the last two weeks of this writing, on June 12, 2016, 49 individuals were killed in a gay club in Orlando, Florida, by an American-born man of Afghan ethnicity professing allegiance to the Islamic State of Iraq and Syria (ISIS) and a hatred of gays. He is an example of how we continue to be separated within a multicultural society. The sad part of this insistence on multiculturalism is that ethnicity continues to separate us on a most fundamental level—psychologically. The issue is not only whether a person of color might need psychological help, but how much safety there is in exposing such a need. How can I trust a therapeutic process where I may be judged and made to feel embarrassed because the cultural cues of the one in power— the therapist or analyst—are not aligned with my cultural foundation? In fact, the conscious training of the Jungian analyst in terms of the classical written works has included studies in which individuals of color have been racially maligned. How does this later express itself within the therapy room? What are the unconscious messages from such a training as regards racism, power, and trust?

The roots of American psychology remain European even though Jungian psychology has borrowed from African and indigenous sources. What does a truly multicultural Jungian psychoanalysis look like? Understanding that racism as a possible archetypal energy is *always* present in the therapy room is a helpful beginning. This establishes a degree of honesty upon which trust can be built.

The sharing of this understanding can exist between therapist and client no matter what the ethnic mix or nonmix of the two. Racial relationships, ethnicity, and racism will eventually be fully present in the room and will need to be acknowledged.

How this happens is yet to be fully written about or engaged in meaningfully except amongst a small group of African American psychoanalysts who completed a video three years ago entitled *Black Analysts Speak*. In addition, over the years, occasional books by African Americans have addressed the therapeutic relationship and the racial relationship that is a part of the clinical work, but this has not occurred within the area of Jungian psychology.

References

Black Psychoanalysts Speak. Accessed at http://www.pep-web.org/document.php?id=pepgrantvs.001.0001a.

Boa, Fraser. (1994). *The Way of the Dream: Conversations on Jungian Dream Interpretation with Marie-Louise von Franz*. Boston, MA: Shambhala.

Heath, Brad, Meghan Hoyer, and Kevin Johnson. *USA Today*, "Local police involved in 400 killings per year." August 15, 2014. Accessed at http://www.usatoday.com/story/news/nation/2014/08/14/police-killings-data/14060357/.

Jung, C. G. (2009). *The Red Book: Liber Novus*. New York: W.W. Norton.

Jung, C. G. (1930/1968). "The complications of American psychology. *Civilization in Transition*". CW 10.

Jung, C. G. (1912/1967). *Symbols of Transformation*. CW 5.

Jung, C. G. (1921/1977). *Psychological Types*. CW 6.

Jung, C. G. (1930/1968). *Civilization in Transition*. CW 10.

Jung, C. G. (1934/1968). *The Archetypes and the Collective Unconscious*. CW 9i.

Jung, C. G. (1935/1976). *The Symbolic Life*. CW 18.

Parham, Thomas A. and Joseph L. White. (1990). *The Psychology of Blacks: An African American Perspective*. Englewood Cliffs, NJ: Prentice Hall.

2
THE REALITY OF RACIAL CHAINS AND THE MYTH OF FREEDOM

In the early 1900s, Jung made three trips to America. The first one, in 1909, was with Freud for a visit to Clark University. The purpose of this visit was to introduce Americans in the field to Freud's type of psychology—psychoanalysis. It was also an opportunity for both men to assess how receptive Americans would be to Freud's ideas regarding the study and implementation of psychoanalysis. In 1912, Jung returned to lecture at Fordham University and to visit with William Alanson White in Washington, and in 1923 he visited a Native American pueblo. He spoke well of his meeting and talks with the tribal chief.

In 1930, Jung wrote a paper first entitled "Your Negroid and Indian Behavior," the title of which was changed to "The Complications of American Psychology" when published as part of the *Collected Works* (CW 10, Para. 946–980). In this paper, Jung goes into detail on his views on African Americans and their relationship with White Americans, noting all of the negative possibilities for Whites because of the "primitive" influences of African Americans:

> The white man is a most terrific *problem* to the Negro, and whenever you affect somebody so profoundly, then, in a mysterious way, something comes back from him to yourself. The Negro by his mere presence is a source of temperamental and mimetic infection, which the European can't help noticing just as much as he sees the hopeless gap between the American and the African negro. Racial infection is a most serious mental and moral *problem* where the primitive outnumbers the white man. America has this *problem* only in a relative degree, because the whites far outnumber the coloured. Apparently he can assimilate the primitive influence with little risk to himself. What would happen if there were a considerable increase in the colored population is another matter.
>
> *(CW 10, Para. 966) (Author italics)*

There appeared to be an overlapping of times and places for many Americans during that period of social unrest in the decade of the 1930s. Americans were uprooted and were moving all over the continent, attempting to find food, shelter, and work following the Wall Street Crash of 1929. Jung had been traveling to America for nearly two decades by the time he wrote the above paper in 1930. What would have influenced him to write such thoughts regarding African Americans? During his 1912 visit, there are no historical facts that suggest that Jung either sought or engaged with any of the African American political, social, or religious leaders of those times (Brewster, 2013). His stated intention to meet with hospitalized African Americans was arranged for him by Alanson White. Jung was able to conduct his 30-day "study" and to obtain the information he sought without expressing any further obligation for what he had obtained from his "subjects."

He notes later in a lecture that it *"did not matter"*; these words of dismissal—*"did not matter"*—have appeared in a revised form as a contemporary rallying call of African American activism, *Black Lives Matter*, because of the most recent killings of African American males by law enforcement officers.

This is a harsh racial reality of African American life then and now: Black lives do not matter to a large segment of American society. This can be viewed from two different perspectives. One is the idea that African American lives do not matter because some say that statistics "prove" that the rate of "Black-on-Black" crimes is higher than the same ratio for White-on-White crimes.

Some have begun to analyze this idea because these statistics appear to always be used in service of showing how African Americans do not care for the lives of those in their racial group.

Another perspective, that of many African Americans and the energetic pull of most recent demonstrations and protests at the deaths of these men, is that Black lives continue to *not* matter to Whites. The use of statistics to show how African Americans kill or harm each other, being more aggressive than other racial groups, appears over time to be a justification for violent, racist actions against all African Americans. When we consider the words and actions raised against African Americans from slavery until the present time, psychologically, most Americans *must* question the value of African American lives.

For African Americans, it is not the questioning of self-worth but rather the constant self-assertion of positive self-value that *must* occupy the daily African American experience. When African American mothers raise their sons, they must support them in being strong, proud, and able to develop a sense of their own self-worth. This is true also for White mothers. But for African American children, the encouragement of these qualities of self-esteem will be placed *against* the collective views held of the society at large. These views, held both consciously and unconsciously, are that African American men are to be feared and mistrusted and that they tend to be violent. They must be ignored and/or feared. The level of deadly violence acted out against African Americans for generations shows this underlying, shadowed thinking in the White collective. Often, the violent force displayed against African Americans in no way matches the small action that caused such a strong reaction by Whites.

In another recent event, a White South Carolina policeman stopped an African American man for a moving violation. The policeman, with his gun drawn, demanded license and registration. The driver of the car leaned into his car to get these items. The policeman moved toward the African American man and shot him. The policeman later reported that he thought the driver of the car was reaching for a gun. Many studies over time have shown the tendency by Whites to project violent behaviors onto African Americans when no violence is intended and when no guns are in the possession of the African American victim. What usually seems apparent to the White observer is that the African American individual is behaving or acting "different." However, there rarely appears to be a way of behaving for African Americans that *is* acceptable. This goes directly to the problem of how African Americans are thought of by Whites, and their perception that it is *us* who have a behavior problem.

In the following quote by Jung from an essay published in 1930, of importance is Jung's lack of *seeing* the African American as an *American*:

> Just as the coloured man lives in your cities and even within your houses, so also he lives under your skin, subconsciously. Naturally it works both ways. Just as every Jew has a Christ complex, so every Negro has a white complex and every American a Negro complex.
>
> *(CW 10, Para. 963)*

This inability to *see* the African American as American is an ongoing, centuries-old problem that continues to hide in the shadows of American racial relations. When will African Americans truly become Americans, be *seen* as Americans? In this instance, Jung is not at fault for stating what both African Americans and Whites feel: the racial tension at being unable to fully claim being American.

This is a major part of the identity problem with *being* African American. It appears forever difficult "settling" into, and claiming, the *American* portion of those two joined words. The above quote by Jung points out the *racial complexes* evident in both races. Jungian psychology has been remiss in exploring the important relevance of these racial complexes, even though their existence was apparent to Jung decades ago. What are the nuances of racial complexes? How would they present themselves in the analytical work between analyst and analysand of different ethnicities or of the same racial background? If every complex has its archetypal center, what would be the archetype(s) for racial complexes?

These are important psychological questions worth exploring as racism and race relations continue to be major and oftentimes volatile problems in America. It is unfortunate for the American Jungian analysts who followed Jung that they have been so reluctant to explore a complex that is still so powerfully present in the clinical setting as well as in the collective. It is interesting to note that every other complex can be explored and amplified by American Jungians with the exception of the *racial complex* first mentioned by Jung. My own analytical training completely avoided the subject. Why this reluctance to delve into this particular complex?

In 1931, Jung wrote "From Mind and Earth" as a part of his continuing series of essays on American culture. There are similarities in the theme of this article with a piece written by Franz Boas, a colleague who explored the influence of the physical environment on the European colonizer.

In developing his own theme, Jung chose African Americans, noting the difference between levels of consciousness—an extremely high level of culture and the primitivity of the unconscious within White Americans, only because of their *living* on shared American soil. He writes:

> The American presents a strange picture: a European with Negro behaviour and an Indian soul. He shares the fate of all usurpers of foreign soil. Certain Australian primitives assert that one cannot conquer foreign soil, because in it there dwell strange ancestor-spirits who reincarnate themselves in the new-born. There is a great psychological truth in this. The foreign land assimilates its conqueror. But unlike the Latin conquerors of Central and South America, the North Americans preserved their European standards with the most rigid puritanism, though they could not prevent the souls of their Indian foes from becoming theirs. Everywhere the virgin earth causes at least the unconscious of the conqueror to sink to the level of its indigenous inhabitants. *Thus, in the American, there is a discrepancy between conscious and unconscious that is not found in the European, a tension between an extremely high conscious level of culture and an unconscious primitivity.*
>
> (CW 10, Para. 103) (Author italics)

Analytical psychology, when transplanted to America, was exclusive in its applicability: it was not intended for African Americans, an idea that is both intriguing and worth exploring. As previously stated, several of Jung's ideas and theories came from indigenous people—some through the work of anthropologists such as Victor Turner and Lucien Lévy-Bruhl. Jung has claimed in his writing that he was just as much a "nigger" because of how he dreamt. It would appear that, similar to other confusions, Jung at first mixed the sociological of race and racism with the psychological of his own complex. There are places in his writing in which he appears genuinely appreciative of Africanist culture and is insightful of what he observes, but this is usually in an abstract, generally noncomplementary way.

However, when he turns to America and race, Jung falls into a racial line of thinking formed and promoted in the days of violent, racist segregation, one that has not been remedied by contemporary American Jungian psychology teaching and training.

It has been decades since Jung wrote his papers regarding African Americans, race, and American racial relations, but many of the issues of racism remain. Jungian psychology is unreceptive to and for African Americans, while other psychologies have succeeded in bringing ethnic groups into their fold. The racial issues that Jung mentioned in his writings are still a deterrent for those of African lineage. It may be too difficult to face the racism of contemporary society and join in analytical psychology on any level while being required to confront the apparent racial bias that runs through Jung's American-directed writings. Perhaps unconsciously, this bias remains in the practice of today's American Jungian psychology.

It is time to face it more directly, if only to lean toward the inclusion of a *third* in a growth toward deepening human consciousness as regards the issue of racial relationships and racial complexes. The opposites that Jung proposed live within our psyches pushes toward a transcendent function third—the resolution of the opposites in service of healing. In some ways, it seems unfair to have an expectation that Jung could have conceived of and created his theoretical model as regards African Americans in any way other than he did.

As with other aspects of his work, Jung delved into the historical facts and developed his theories oftentimes based on current events or present-day collective needs. The contemporary American life that Jung visited, though he never resided in it, was one of racial bias, active racial violence, and an American consciousness that was still extricating itself from not only slavery, but also from the belief that slavery was and should be an acceptable aspect of American life. Post Civil War, plantations and thousands of acres of land were still worked by the children and grandchildren of slaves. African Americans were still being lynched, were unschooled for the most part, and were treated as societal "outcasts."

New eruptions of anti-immigration bias came in waves with each arrival of immigrants, but the prejudice against African Americans remained intact no matter how many other ethnic groups arrived. The mere existence of African Americans proved to be intolerable to many White Americans, even in the post-Reconstruction period of America's history.

In *Slavery by Another Name: The Re-Enslavement of Black Americans from the Civil War to World War II*, author Douglas Blackmon (2009) gives the reader an in-depth look at the lives of African American men and women. Those who survived slavery and Southern plantations were only forced into a different kind of slavery. In his introductory chapter, Blackmon tells the story of one such African American, Green Cottenham, who was arrested by the sheriff in Shelby County, Alabama. He was 22 years of age. Blackmon says,

> Cottenham had committed no true crime. *Vagrancy*, the offense of a person not being able to prove at a given moment that he or she is employed ... was capriciously enforced by local sheriffs ... and most tellingly in a time of massive umemployment among all southern men, was reserved almost exclusively for black men. Cottenham's offense was blackness.
>
> (Blackmon, 2009, p. 1)

The next day, Cottenham, the youngest of nine children born to former slaves in an adjoining county, was sold. Under a standing arrangement between the county and a vast subsidiary of the industrial titan of the North—U.S. Steel Corporation—the sheriff turned the young man over to the company for the duration of his sentence. In return, the subsidiary, Tennessee Coal, Iron & Railroad Company, gave the county $12.00 a month to pay off Cottenham's fine and fees. What the company's managers did with Cottenham, and the thousands of Black men they purchased from sheriffs across Alabama, was entirely up to them (p. 1).

Green Cottenham's story only begins one phase as he is handed over to the mining company. Men in his position had no power to speak of their innocence or any legal rights that could protect them with any true sense of justice because of their race. Once thrown into the Pratt Mines near Birmingham, "he was chained inside a long wooden barrack at night and required to spend nearly every waking hour digging and loading coal.... Cottenham was subject to the whip for failure to dig the requisite amount, at risk of physical torture for disobedience, and vulnerable to the sexual predations of other miners." This took place in 1908, 43 years after the American Civil War.

When Jung was writing his papers in 1930 and 1931 on America and the influence of Africa Americans on American society, African American men were still imprisoned on chain gangs. This alternative way of enslaving the men, as with Cottenham's "re-enslavement" almost 20 years before, proved a powerful way for Whites to continue having free African American labor under a system without justice or mercy. Some say that modern-day prisons have replaced the chain gangs.

Blackmon continues in Chapter 17, focusing on the overreaching power of chain gangs. He writes:

> Contrary to the congratulatory pronouncements that followed Georgia's "abolition" of the practice of selling Black prisoners in 1908, the state had more forced labor slaves than ever by 1930. In excess of 8,000 men—nearly all of them Black—worked in chain gangs in 116 counties. Of 1.1 million African Americans in the state that year, approximately half lived under the direct control and force of whites—unable to move or seek employment elsewhere under threat that to do so would lead to the dreaded chain gang.
> (Blackmon, 2009, p. 371)

As we review and highlight the life experiences of African Americans during the historical time period of the 1930s during which Jung visited and wrote about America, we can ask whether it is possible that he knew so little about the true nature of the psychological and physical suffering of most African Americans? If this is *not* true, then what did he know and how did he come to his conclusions about African Americans, having only spent 30 days with the men at St. Elizabeth Hospital? Jung's writing can be helpful to us in understanding further his thinking about African Americans. It might also help us understand the racial lineage the American Jungian analyst continues to live within our multicultural society. From *The Complications of American Psychology*:

> You see this particularly in the American sex problem as it had developed since the war. There is a marked tendency to promiscuity, which shows

not only in the frequency of divorces but quite particularly in the peculiar liberation from sex prejudices in the younger generation.... The most recent developments in the field of sexual morality tend toward sexual *primitivity*, analogous to the instability of the moral habits of *primitive* people, where under the influence of collective emotion all sex taboos instantly disappear.

(CW 10, Para. 958)

Jung's words remind one of the racial overtones of sexual promiscuity that have always been projected onto African Americans. This aversion to claiming one's own sexuality has also been a Shadow issue for the White American collective since before slavery. Sexual violence through the rape, molestation, and physical abuse of African women during and following slavery has been well documented (Giddings, 1988).

An illness of the body, such as AIDS, was initially believed to originate in Africa. The weight of racial scorn was directed toward African Americans: men for their supposed sexual prowess and women for their sexual promiscuity.

During the fearful years of the first AIDS outbreak, individuals with AIDS were publically shamed and many times denied their most basic human rights because of having contracted the virus. The push for these civil rights in the face of the devastating number of deaths in gay and African American communities brought a new realization of the need for and protection of the rights of patients. The social fight to obtain medical services for African Americans during the AIDS epidemic spoke to racially biased prejudice. A book that addresses this and other aspects of AIDS as related to African Americans is Jacob Levenson's *The Secret Epidemic: The Story of AIDS and Black America* (2005).

The belief that African Americans, both men and women, are more sexually active and oriented and have radically different sexual desires and behaviors than Whites was one of the ideas driving the Tuskegee Study. This was the formal investigation and attempt to *document* a popular racist belief. The informal manner in which the belief continued can be seen in the writings and language of American social scientists and psychologists and also in the writings of Jung.

A century ago, there were minimal laws to protect patients. The impetus was on the doctors, nurses, and hospital staff to provide this protection, in many cases leaving patients vulnerable to any number of "studies" that were to the patient's disadvantage. One instance of such violations of patients' rights—those of African American patients—came with the case of the Tuskegee Syphilis Study, which was conducted from 1932 until 1972. When Jung returned to America in 1937 for the Terry Lectures at Yale, the Tuskegee Study had been in progress for 5 years. During the 40-year period of the "study," 600 African American men were enrolled in a program that was supposedly for the treatment of a medical condition called "bad blood" or syphilis. At the start of the program, 399 of the men had the disease, while 201 had no signs of the disease.

The purported purpose of the study was to help the men, but the underlying agenda was a study of African American sexual behaviors. Some men in the study were never explicitly told they had syphilis. The participants in the studies were given a financial allowance, shelter, and free medical care. The intention of the "study" appeared to be to establish a "rule" or "theory" regarding African American sexual activity, which was considered to be more important than the protection of the men's lives or those of their sexual partners.

The study was seeking to show that sex was more important to these men than life, because they did not stop having sexual relations with their partners while knowing they were sick with "bad blood." However, the researchers conducting the study did not *tell* the men the true nature of their study and allowed the men with the disease to go untreated long after the discovery of penicillin in 1946. This known cure for syphilis was withheld from the research subjects until 1972 when the study's existence became known through a newspaper story.

During this 40-year period, men were given the disease of syphilis, their wives and female sexual partners were exposed to syphilis, and their children were born with congenital syphilis. The result of this immense violation of the rights of African Americans resulted in the creation of the Office of Human Research Protection in 1976. This agency became the overseeing organization for granting patients legal rights while being research subjects.

This aspect of American healthcare, especially the care of the mentally ill, increased in importance by the time of the AIDS epidemic of the 1980s.

During the years of Jung's writing on African Americans in the 1930s and the racial problem that Whites had with the mere existence of African Americans, the latter were being systematically made ill and died because of an American government-approved racist-driven "research" program. These were also the years when Jung was involved with the politics of Nazism and its effects on the psychoanalytical movement in Zurich.

His attention would not have been taken up for any good length of time with American social affairs as he would have been too engaged with the events occurring in Europe during the decade of the 1930s. Maybe there was a connection that we have never heard about between Jung's racially provocative language regarding African Americans during this time and the rise of Nazism with its racist edicts against Jews.

Jung's writing regarding African Americans generally focused on the negative or absence of *attributes* of their culture. In Jung's day and in line with his experiences of Americans, and during those historically close-to-slavery times, it was unthinkable that African Americans actually *had* a culture. Most of the clearly Afro-centric inheritances that existed in the twentieth century were discounted by American society at large.

Whatever was appreciated was usually done as a joke or in a back-handed manner. In one of his very few (what he thought to be) "appreciations" of African Americans, Jung made such an observation when having dinner with an American family during his 1909 visit. He had joked that he fully expected to see black fingerprints on his plate, which was set down on the table by a young Black man.

None of the Whites laughed or appeared to enjoy this, but Jung expressed his happiness when the African American server laughed out loud:

> It was the Negro servant, and it was the real American laughter, that grand, unrestrained, unsophisticated laugher revealing rows of teeth, tongue, palate, everything, just a trifle exaggerated perhaps and certainly less than sixteen years old. How I loved that African brother.
>
> *(CW 10, Para. 950)*

Jung could "love" this young man because the young man gave Jung what *he* required—laughter and an appreciation for *his* joke. What might have happened if the young man had attempted to engage Jung in a more serious conversation? Though this possibility is unlikely, the obvious positioning of power is in Jung's favor. This is true not only because he is the guest, but also because he is White and his server is African American. It is interesting to note from the above quote that even though Jung calls the laughter "American," he calls the young man "African." In this ironic, unexpected way, Jung has identified and joined the African with the American.

Jung barely referred to *racial complexes*. No American Jungian analyst or writer developed his thoughts regarding this particular complex. Might these racial complexes also include or be a part of cultural complexes? American culture at the turn of the twentieth century was still divided between the assumed sophistication of the eastern United States and the "roughness" of the west. African Americans were still attempting to find their place post-slavery in what was already purported to be a multicultural society. Back then as now, African Americans were still trying to work out the details of such a claim.

The identity of African Americans, enmeshed as a part of their psychological being, must continually work to strengthen and own a culture that has been stolen, disrespected, and disregarded. This identity became even more precious during the early 1960s, when voices shouting "Black Power," with the demand for the respectability of African America culture, rose to prominence in the minds of the American collective. This period of time caused an influential change in the consciousness of many Americans, both African American and White, as to the significance of African American culture.

American slavery has had an exceedingly traumatic effect on African Americans and their ability to rest comfortably within an African American identity. The stripping away of African rituals and language alone has been a most obvious tragedy for African Americans. There is something in the African American psyche that continues to long for those things of the motherland that can no longer be directly obtained. The language that has kept alive a sense of knowing and belonging is disappearing more and more frequently as African countries fight internally over tribal differences, money, and natural resources. The imagination of the African American must struggle to remember and create new rituals from what can be recalled from those ancient times.

In attempting this recollection, there is an ongoing struggle to feel safe in what can be newly created in honor of what is past, and what can emerge with a sense of freedom. One of the hallmarks of trusting one's identity as an adult is accepting that the environment in which you have grown up reflects the truth of who you really are. This is usually possible for African Americans, but the truth is somewhat split.

The psychological stress of always having to accommodate a White Other, one that can place unreasonable and unworthy demands on one, appears at times to lead African Americans into a dissociated state as regards identity. Though Jung does not say this directly, it seems that his words regarding racial complexes could be interpreted in this way. He does conclude his quote about racial complexes by stating, "As a rule the coloured man would give anything to change his skin, and the white man hates to admit that he has been touched by the black."

The cultural complexes we develop as a result of our genetic ancestry, the physical environment in which we are raised, and the impress of the American collective are decidedly "touched" by racial makeup. Jung was correct in this assessment. I'm certain that there are times when an African American would be more than willing to "change his skin," to change his condition to those of pre-slavery days. Who would want to travel across the Atlantic Ocean spooned with thousands of captured souls in the belly of a slave ship, ripped from everything one has known about life? When Jung says this regarding the changing of skin color, I do not believe he truly understood the sorrow and the strength of living through what centuries of African Americans had already endured.

It might appear that the other part of Jung's statement is also correct. There were many White Americans in Jung's time, as well as over the last 100 years since Jung first came to America, who "hate" that they have felt the "touch" of the Black man.

This is one of the most important underlying Shadow reasons for segregation—the avoidance of becoming/being in touch with the Other—of going *primitive*. But it is important to note here that *touching* by Whites, when for their own purposes, has always been acceptable. That purpose might be rape or torture or some form of punishment. The idea is that the control and power of who could do the touching rested with Whites.

The truth about our multicultural society is that we cannot avoid one another. No matter how much we wish to exchange our skin color and avoid one another, both of which Jung noted, American multiculturalism must continue to engage with the battle of working out the archetypal issue of racism and the Opposites.

African American culture has always been under scrutiny from the early days of slavery until present times. When a people arrive to America's shores, as did the first Africans, there are decades of getting one's self "situated." Unlike other arriving Americans, enslaved Africans did not choose to come to America. Thus the sensibilities of power and choice involved were absent. There was no planning to leave Africa in anticipation of beginning a new life. Africans were not willing immigrants.

Upon arrival, they were relegated to the lowest social status and remained there for centuries. America has not released its power to control, scrutinize, and diminish African Americans. American slavery and its continuing centuries-old wish to control African Americans has proven difficult to change. I believe that the incarceration of African American men and their violent deaths at the hands of American policemen continues to show the acting out of this collective wish to control.

The White American collective oftentimes prides itself on its ability to make radical changes in American society. Perhaps there is worthiness to this self-acclamation. The election of Barack Obama as president was seen as a shift in the American consciousness as related to race. It was a definitive moment in American history. I think it showed the imprint of the collective upon the archetypal. However, it appears that the backlash from such a shift has been severe, for African American males in particular.

Is this a compensatory movement in the American psyche—we have an African American in the White House, therefore more African American young men (who the president says would look like *his* son) must die?

The president's identification with young African American men who were killed by law enforcement made many Whites angry. They appeared almost enraged that the president could claim a common identity with those young men. Why is this so? Why is it unacceptable for the president to align himself with the sons who died and the mothers who have lost their sons? This also seems like an aspect of the American Shadow as regards race. One of the features of African American life is that we will claim others from our culture who are not blood relatives. Perhaps this is as a result of slavery, but it is also a feature of African community life. Individuals who are not blood relatives can become a part of a clan or lineage if they are without immediate family. It may also relate to our cultural archetypal DNA, which says we understand that we are part of a group—not always isolated individuals, striving for an American rugged individualism.

Slavery forced Africans to leave sisters, brothers, mothers—all of whom had been family. American slavery tore families apart in the most brutal of ways. There may still be something in the White American psyche that cannot tolerate the idea that African Americans can finally have control over their own family relations. When the president made his statement claiming one of the killed young men, Michael Brown, as a son, the racist energy for dividing African Americans pushed forward into our visible lives. The rage of those against the president's position was palpable. There were many voices raised against him for identifying with Michael Brown as father to son. The twenty-first century is a time when African Americans continue to confront with more intensity the issue of racism.

The resurgence of protest demonstrations, slogans that call Americans to action against what many consider racist killings, and the apparent never-ending struggle for African American civil rights all lay claim to the fact of continued racism in the American collective. African Americans are still engaged in political and social battle for recognition of an identity that *does matter*. This appears to be the core issue of current antagonisms, but it is not a new issue in terms of the fight for African American civil liberties. These liberties definitely include the right to live a psychologically sound existence without the always-looming terror of harm or even death because of racism. After several centuries, African Americans are still attempting to strengthen their sense of identity and of being American without racist prejudice and rejection.

Jung was correct—American psychology *is* complicated—still. Perhaps he saw the impending difficulties of a successful integration of his analytical psychology due to the issue of American race relations. Perhaps he added his voice on the side of what looked right (perhaps because of his theory of primitive psychology?). It is apparent that the complications remain, and those of us who sit in offices doing psychoanalytical work can wish for more ease in terms of racial relations and racism.

Somehow, however, there seems the possibility of finding peace in an intercultural way for the practice of analytical psychology, even with its clearly racist beginnings. How we manage this will depend in large part on how we are able to accept the cultural attributes of the other.

References

Blackmon, Douglas A. (2009). *Slavery by Another Name: The Re-Enslavement of Black Americans from the Civil War to World War II*. New York: Random House.

Brewster, Fanny. (2013). "Wheel of fire: The African American dreamer and cultural consciousness." *Jung Journal: Culture and Psyche*, v. 7, issue 1, pp. 70–87.

Giddings, Paula. (1988). *When and Where I Enter: The Impact of Black Women on Race and Sex in America*. New York: Bantam.

Jung, C. G. (2009). *The Red Book: Liber Novus*. New York: W.W. Norton.

Jung, C. G. (1930/1968). "The complications of American psychology." *Civilization in Transition*. CW 10.

Jung, C. G. (1912/1967). *Symbols of Transformation*. CW 5.

Jung, C. G. (1921/1977). *Psychological Types*. CW 6.

Jung, C. G. (1930/1968). *Civilization in Transition*. CW 10.

Jung, C. G. (1934/1968). *The Archetypes and the Collective Unconscious*. CW 9i.

Jung, C. G. (1935/1976). *The Symbolic Life*. CW 18. (CH1)

Levenson, Jacob. (2005). *The Secret Epidemic: The Story of AIDS and Black America*. New York: Random House.

3
AMERICAN RACIAL BLACK AND WHITE COMPLEXES

In "A Review of the Complex Theory," Jung states:

> Fear of complexes is a bad signpost, however, because it always points away from the unconscious and back into consciousness. Complexes are something so unpleasant that nobody in his right senses can be persuaded that the motive forces which maintain them could betoken anything good.
>
> *(CW 8, Para. 211)*

When we consider Jung's words in this quote in relationship to the *racial complex*, we can see how difficult it might be to initiate an engagement of dialogue with this complex as a theme. In his work on the complex, Jung says that the complex is only a representative part of our psyche but that it is an important part. The complex is usually beyond our control and develops from not only our individual personality but also from the environment in which we grow up. The psychic nature of the complex defies a strict definition and, like the archetype, it can present us with bursts of energy that can appear beyond the ego's conscious control. Jung says of the complexes that we might know we have them but it is more likely "that complexes can have us" (para. 210).

Many times what has been written about by African American authors—Ralph Ellison, for example, in *Invisible Man*; or Richard Wright in *Black Boy*—may be aspects of Black and White racial complexes. Both of these African American literary classics have as their theme the emotionality of main characters attempting to resolve issues of an activated racial complex. One notes that even though, as with parental complexes or guilt complexes, we can see that we have this complex, knowledge is insufficient to resolve the tension of our complexes.

Jung indicates in his chapter on complex theory that we must somehow transform the complex, not only intellectually through careful consideration, but also, perhaps even more importantly, through an emotional release that joins understanding of the complex with this release.

It seems that Jung was actually giving American Jungians an opportunity to investigate our American racial complexes when he spoke of them in "The Complications of American Psychology." I do believe that he understood not only the complications but the extreme quagmire of even beginning to unravel and peer into the depths of the American racial complexes of both Whites and Blacks.

In addressing the racial complex from an African American cultural perspective through the writings of Ellison and Wright, there is the necessary White complex to consider. Jung says that each one has the racial complex of the other—White and Black complexes exist in the opposite of the Other. This being so, how does the White complex further show itself in African Americans? Both main characters from these writings are confronted with racial inequality and live in a racially unjust society in which their color causes them to suffer. These characters represent millions of African Americans who have *actually* suffered because of their skin color. This is not the "neurotic" suffering of which Jung speaks, in defining the activity of an ego that wishes to avoid the painful suffering of the psychological work of seeing and dealing with complexes. The idea that African Americans can feel themselves invisible, ignored, and even tortured for being African Americans does speak to what could develop in the African American psyche as a White complex within the personal unconscious.

This complex, if Jung is correct, can live a quiet existence in the unconscious unless brought to life by psychic associations within the unconscious. The personal unconscious then becomes numinously active, awakening the complex. The ego that mediates—if it can—the anxieties aroused by the awakened complex struggles to gain control over the impact of emotion pushing through into consciousness.

An important question here might be how the African American ego can mediate the constant threat of racially inspired violence and death while being vulnerable and open to the intense emotions of the racial complex, which must be reconciled in order to restore a psychic balance.

This is but one of many questions that must be asked if we truly want to investigate American Jungian psychology. It and other questions have been dormant a very long time—almost like the complexes themselves, activated only by a psychic "push" to come into consciousness. I would suggest that racial complexes are some of the most "unpleasant" ones. In the previous quote, Jung tells us that complexes are unpleasant. He is not referring specifically to racial complexes but rather to all complexes.

Jung states the following in his discussion of the psychic disruption that can be caused by a complex: "An active complex puts us momentarily under a state of duress, of compulsive thinking and acting, for which under certain conditions the only appropriate term would be the judicial concept of diminished responsibility" (CW 8, Para. 200). In turning to the Black complex that Jung believed existed in White Americans, we can see how the racial violence so oftentimes projected onto African Americans can exist in Whites as well.

When Jung speaks of the state of "duress … compulsive thinking and acting," I am reminded of the recent death of nine African Americans who were murdered in their Charleston, South Carolina, church during a prayer meeting by Dylann Roof, a 21-year-old White man.

Roof said that he wanted to kill them because of his "hatred" of African Americans. He said he *wanted to start a race war*. His is considered a hate crime. Might we say that his actions, based on his own words and thoughts, prompted by a Black complex under duress, led him to such an act of "diminished responsibility"?

The powerful possible damage of our racial complexes to us as individuals, and to others as well, must be acknowledged. Jung acknowledges that we can never resolve, as in remove, complexes from our unconscious experiences. Our work as American Jungians is to first acknowledge them and from there continue to integrate the emotions that must result from them in this recognition. When we cannot do this psychological work, we have racial conflicts like those that have continued in American society for centuries. However, if American Jungians do not ever even mention the words *racial complexes*, it is impossible for our community consciousness to increase our own knowledge and understanding of how to add our collective voices to a process of discovery.

If Dylann Roof's ego was so overwhelmed by his Black racial complex, then we could say that he over-identified with his complex. This over-identification led him into a psychotic state where he saw himself as part of a national Aryan movement—a savior for the White "race."

The projections that he put forth toward African Americans consisted of the personal unconscious material of his complex. It is important to note that African Americans were the recipients of these hostile projections. I believe that this is one possible outcome of Jung's ideas regarding his complex theory. I have extended his idea of the racial complex to one natural conclusion when psychosis overtakes neurosis.

It should be noted that in Jung's chapter "A Review of the Complex Theory," he did not refrain from referring to "primitive peoples." Within the context of this theory and others more broadly, "primitives" reside in that place of the unconscious—unable to recognize much difference between the conscious and that which belongs to the unconscious. According to Jung, in relationship to the complex, this is true because ego consciousness is overpowered by the unconscious material of the complex. When this occurs, the rational mind cannot function in its full capacity in terms of guidance and good judgment. An example was previously cited regarding Dylann Roof. This possession of ego consciousness can also happen on a group level.

When Jung references the Ku Klux Klan as simply being a part of a social group, I think he misses the activation of the Black racial complex inherent in the psyches of these participants. The white robes in which they enshrine themselves are a metaphor for the overcoming of their egos, which are now completely shrouded in the darkness of the unconscious. When the Black Power Movement of the 1960s erupted and the Black Panther movement took force in America, its members prided themselves on dressing in black. Black became the symbolic color of power in that decade as it had previously been denigrated in all the previous ones. The activation of a White racial complex led to the rise of individuals asserting power and control in an ego-conscious manner.

As previously stated, Jung notes that we can alleviate suffering from our complexes by acknowledging their presence and feeling our emotions as discharged by the psychic energy of the complex. The Panther party members became "visible" through voice and action, engaging in what for many of them had only been realized on a personal unconscious level, if considered from the perspective of Jung's complex theory.

The Opposites of group racial conflict became alive and at work on a more conscious level as Americans continued into the decade of the 1960s and early 1970s. As we engage in the politics of the 2016 American presidential election, we can perhaps see this racial conflict once enlivened on the group level of the 1960s.

One of the significant aspects of Jung's complex theory is that he appears to understand the importance of the complexes for psychic healing. It is through their recognition and activation that we confront and deal with emotional places of "stuckness." Learning about and delving into the painful issues of reconciling one's parental complexes helps provide the individual with a sort of psychic peace, which Jung believes can only come from seeing the elusive complex. We cannot know ourselves, heal ourselves, unless we know our complexes and are willing to take the path toward healing. Of course, this healing is a lifelong work because complexes never go away. We can never rid ourselves of the psychic energy that helps create them or drive them. Since complexes are a part of the natural occurrence of psychic life, we must look to what Jung has often called "adaptation." He uses this word to describe the work being done with patients who come for analysis. The brief time they may be in analysis allows for ego strengthening in service of a more cooperative relationship between the ego and the unconscious.

The recognition of personal complexes, including racial ones and the Shadow, can make up a great deal of the psychological work for changing consciousness. A large part of our work as American Jungians is to delve more deeply, creating a better understanding of the racial complexes of which Jung spoke.

Unlike in his studies of dreams or alchemy, Jung did not provide us with much of his thinking regarding racial complexes. It appears to me that this is truly the work of post-Jungians. Since we have a belief in psyche and the ability to take an attitude of discovery, of "not knowing," we are always in the field of questioning. The questions that I include in this writing regarding racial complexes are inquiries into achieving a deeper understanding of this particular aspect of our collective psyche.

Jung, in speaking of a patient who believed he had cancer in spite of Jung's attempts to change the patient's thinking, states, "Complexes do indeed behave like secondary or partial personalities possessing a mental life of their own.... Many complexes are split off from consciousness because the latter preferred to get rid of them by repression but there are others that have never been in consciousness" (CW 11, Para. 21–22). Jung appears to assume that our American racial complexes are, or should be, known to us in the same way as with the complex of Opposites between Christians and Jews. How might we think of this to better understand the racial complexes of White and Black within a Jungian context? If both American Whites and Blacks can believe that they share a racial complex, how does this understanding support an increase in a better fellowship between ethnic groups rather than animosity?

Perhaps there is a lack of knowledge and belief in the very idea of a shared racial complex. One of the features of the complex is its duality in terms of being both negative and positive. In this duality of the Opposites, the duality of the complex, each holder of a complex projects the negative onto the other, contending that they are the "problem." This is what appears to have happened to W. E. B. Du Bois many times in his own lifetime—that because of his color, he was the "problem." I believe this to be a group projection rather than simply that of an individual. Within each individual ego consciousness, and most often with the collective group consciousness, there is a belief that the Other is the negative. When this gets acted out, embodied in the society, racism as a collective experience comes to the forefront.

During the course of the 2016 American presidential election, the presumptive nominee of the Republican Party has indicated that he was being selectively persecuted by a particular judge of Mexican ancestry for the simple reason that he was of Mexican ancestry. A political firestorm erupted because of the inherent racism of the nominee's comments. The nominee refused to refute his statement and held fast to his position that he was being "unfairly" treated by the American-born federal judge.

I think that as Americans we have a great difficulty seeing how racism lives in our consciousness. Yes, Jung could see these complexes, but I'm not so certain *we* all can see with such clarity. In fact, one of the elements of racism in America is that those of us with White complexes, in this case African Americans, for the most part are like Ellison's character—we are invisible to Whites in the society. When we do become visible, we are *the* problem. This is repeated over and over again—if it wasn't for us, African Americans, there would be no social or political problems in America.

In the throes of the American election primary campaign, we have seen and heard barely concealed racial issues gradually emerge to reach a pitched point of heated discussion. This is as it should be. The American collective is once again bringing into consciousness a racial complex that exists on both individual as well as a collective level. These are the conversations we as Jungian analysts must begin to engage, worry over, and attempt to integrate.

The popularity of the Republican Party's nominee has been greatly attributed to his call to "make America great again." Many have pointed out that these "great" times were when there was mass oppression of African Americans socially, politically, and educationally. The majority of individuals who have voted in the primary elections for the Republican Party nominee are White males. There is almost a complete lack of racial diversity within the Republican Party. This continues to be a major problem for this American political party, whose most historically important early party leader, Abraham Lincoln, freed African American slaves.

In his essay "The Psychological Foundation of Belief in Spirits," Jung says:

> Certain complexes arise on account of painful or distressing experiences in a person's life, experiences of an emotional nature which leave lasting psychic wounds behind them. A bad experience of this sort often crushes valuable qualities in an individual. All these produce unconscious complexes of a personal nature. A primitive would rightly speak of a loss of soul, because certain portions of psyche have indeed disappeared.
> (CW 11, Para. 594)

In addressing the last line of the above quote, it might at first be important to note that the recognition of a loss of soul might also be apparent to a *White* person.

This example of "splitting" along racial lines reinforces the experience of racial Opposites within Jungian psychology. Returning to the opening sentence of the above quote, I focus on Jung's idea of "lasting psychic wounds" and suggest that the aforementioned "splitting" is a further example of this type of wounding. African Americans, I think, have certainly had a life of "necessary" splitting due to racial trauma caused by racism.

As African American children, we learn at an early age the importance of self-identification by skin color. In the racially segregated small South Carolina town in which I spent my early formative years, an understanding of social "place" based on Southern racial rules was imperative. I learned at an early age that I could only drink at the *Colored Only* water fountain, sit in the *Colored Only* movie theater balcony and attend the *Colored Only* elementary school. The punishment for breaking these rules could be a severe beating or even death if you were an African American adult. How does this kind of existence not "crush" the "valuable qualities" of individuals—of entire generations?

I suggest that because of the strength of racial complexes, unacknowledged over centuries, these complexes continue to haunt us. Our inability to bring further into consciousness the reality of the existence of these racial complexes, especially within our own Jungian communities, only adds to the complicity of repression. And so we wait until the next racially motivated mass shooting, beating, or killing by a uniformed officer of an African American. These complexes seem to be constellated during this time period as they were in our not-so-distant past in the late twentieth century.

I trust that Jung was correct in his belief that we cannot rid ourselves of our complexes. They are an intricate part of our psychic map. Since we cannot eliminate them, how do we bring sufficient attention to them without constantly activating the negative pole of the racial complex, bringing more psychological and perhaps physical trauma? We do not know exactly how our racial complexes work, what makes them work—how to even think about making them function more in the interest of morality, personal transformation, or individuation. Perhaps, the best way forward or downward as American Jungians is to first do what Jung did, and say the words *racial complexes*.

References

Ellison, R. (1953/1989). *Invisible Man*. New York: Vintage Books.
Jung, C. G. (2009). *The Red Book: Liber Novus*. New York: W.W. Norton.
Jung, C. G. (1930/1968). "The complications of American psychology." *Civilization in Transition*. CW 10.
Jung, C. G. (1912/1967). *Symbols of Transformation*. CW 5.
Jung, C. G. (1921/1977). *Psychological Types*. CW 6.
Jung, C. G. (1934/1968). *The Archetypes and the Collective Unconscious*. CW 9i.
Wright, Richard. (1945/2007). *Black Boy*. New York: Harper Perennial Modern Classics.

4
AFRICANIST TRADITIONS AND AFRICAN AMERICAN CULTURE

The Grace of God

The canoe pushes
against midnight blue water
our heads bow
will fish
silent stars
look into our eyes
give us a promise of hope
only the canoe timber listens
creaks out its own story of journey
from the inland forest
knowing no other life
cut from its roots
leaving the others
still standing tall
branch fingers
infinitely
reaching upward
the river
accepts the canoe's tears
making them its own
holding the wood spirit gently
keeping it afloat
all the while guiding us
its human cargo to that
impatient ship

> the Grace of God
> sitting in night's darkest shadow
> ship sails
> unfurl
> hit the wind,
> circles of water
> rise, slap the ship's bottom
> our fettered feet plant deeper
> into the canoe
> fighting the journey to come
> fighting the Grace of God
>
> *Fanny Brewster*
> Journey: The Middle Passage

The Transference

Jung has spoken of *the Transference* as one of the most significant aspects of Jungian psychology. It is largely due to this exchange of conscious and unconscious psychic material—energy—that the analysand is able to find healing. The analyst is connected into the circle of healing, growth, and knowledge. In *The Psychology of the Transference*, Jung discusses the Transference in relationship to alchemy. Each person—analyst and analysand—must be touched by the work and feel the spirit of the work or nothing happens to create a transformative psychological experience.

> The Transference, however, alters the psychological stature of the doctor, though this is at first imperceptible to him. He too becomes affected and has as much difficulty in distinguishing between the patient and what has taken possession of him as has the patient himself. This leads both, in time, to a direct confrontation with the demonic forces lurking in the darkness. The resultant paradoxical blend of positive and negative, of trust and fear, of hope and doubt, of attraction and repulsion, is characteristic of the initial relation.
> (CW 16, Para. 375)

Parallel experiences include those matching Jung's healing practices that are present from African traditions. It is well documented that traditional healers from African societies had a prominent role in the care of members of the village, clan, and tribe. This relationship was one in which it was recognized by both parties, patient and healer, that there were other entities—spirits, God, who had brought on the sickness.

In this same vein, it was imagined that the ability to be healed would come from not only the efforts of the healer but also the spiritual intention of the patient. Therefore, both healer and patient joined their psychic energies together in the act of re-creating health. The healer was expected to be a knowledgeable member of society. This ability to understand what was happening in the lives of members of the community gave the healer a better understanding of the psychological problems affecting his or her patient.

There is an exchange of energy that happens between patient and healer that infuses the relationship with the necessary "spirit" or god energy for healing. In speaking about this aspect of healing amongst the Yoruba, which is very much intertwined with religion, author E. Thomas Lawson in *Religions of Africa* says:

> The role of the specialist in medicine is very similar to that in the Zulu system. Though all Yoruba have knowledge of medicine, the *oloogun*, the specialist in identifying the causes and prescribing the cures for the various illnesses that beset the Yoruba, plays a key role. He is the repository of medicinal knowledge. What is particularly interesting is that he usually works in cooperation with the babalawo, for it is he as diviner who is supposed to be particularly adept at uncovering the reasons for an illness. But medicine is not an autonomous system. Its power comes from the gods. *In that sense the oloogun is a conduit for healing power.*
> (Lawson, 1984, p. 56)

The alchemical energies of Jung's transference are not unlike the presence and activation of that energy happening within the relationship between the African healer and patient. In both circumstances, there is an understanding that something else is alive and is promoting healing. Within the Jungian context, it is the unconscious material seeking to become known to the ego of the analyst and vice versa.

The mutuality of this relationship is what helps to deepen an understanding of the patient's problem—the reason that brought him to therapy.

Mana personalities are present, creating more psychic energy in the field and awakening and alerting patient and therapist to healing potentialities. Within an African context, the patient is known to have more physical features that show themselves—increased body temperature, a deeper depression, a discontinuance of sleep. It is clear within both settings that a different energy becomes present between the two individuals as the work proceeds.

In *African Religions and Philosophy*, John Mbiti says the following:

> First and foremost, medicine-men are concerned with sickness, disease and misfortune. In African societies these are generally believed to be caused by the ill-will of one person against another.... The medicine-man has therefore to discover the cause of the sickness, find out who the criminal is, diagnose the nature of the disease, apply the right treatment and supply a means of preventing the misfortune from occurring again. This is the process that medicine-men follow in dealing with illness and misfortune: it is partly psychological and partly physical. Thus, the medicine-man applies both physical and "spiritual" (or psychological) treatment, which assures the sufferer that all is and will be well.
> (Mbiti, 1989, p. 165)

One of our earliest understandings of the priest, healer, or medicine-man came from the Egyptians through the Egyptian Mystery System. There has been an ongoing academic battle for years as to the viability of Egypt as African and as the place from which Greek philosophy and its cultural arts originated. In *Stolen Legacy: Greek Philosophy Is Stolen Egyptian Philosophy*, author George G. M. James, discussing the taking of Egyptian intellectual artifacts to Greece, says,

> In the drama of Greek philosophy there are three actors, who have played distinct parts, namely Alexander the Great, who by an act of aggression invaded Egypt in 333 B.C. and ransacked and looted the Royal Library at Alexandria and together with his companions carried off a booty of scientific, philosophic and religious books. Egypt was then stolen and annexed as a portion of Alexander's empire; but the invasion plan included far more than mere territorial expansion; *for it prepared the way and made it possible for the capture of the culture of the African Continent.* This brings us to the second actor, that is the School of Aristotle whose students moved from Athens to Egypt and converted the royal library, first into a research centre, and secondly into a University and thirdly compiled that vast body of scientific knowledge which they had gained from research, together with the oral instructions which Greek students had received from the Egyptian priests, into what they have called the history of Greek Philosophy.
> (James, 1992, p. 153–154)

The above quote by James is significant because it establishes a line of thought further back than Jung or even the Greeks. The individuals responsible for healing in Egypt were trained priests who developed their healing art on the African continent. In expanding how we might conceive of modern day analysts, going back to the beginning, let's look again at what James states:

> According to Herodotus, the Egyptian Priests possessed super-natural powers, for they had been trained in the esoteric philosophy of the greater Mysteries, and were experts in magic. They had the power of controlling the minds of men (hypnosis), the power of predicting the future (prophecy), and the power over nature, (i.e., the power of Gods) by giving commands in the name of the Divinity and accomplishing great deeds.
> (James, 1992, p. 134)

This description of Egyptian priests, though highly infused with attributes, is what we come to expect on an unconscious level and what was actually purported to be happening on another energetic level between analyst and analysand. There was a magic, an alchemical experience that could and would happen in the relationship. It is interesting to see that what "possessed" the healer began in the African culture, traveled to Europe, and eventually arrived in the Americas.

In the early days of slavery, African Americans were treated by medicine-men and women healers from African villages. The waters of the ocean, lakes and streams were all designated as sacred. Oftentimes, spiritual healers made pilgrimages to these locations in order to obtain such sacred water for performing rituals. The importance of such rituals is noted by Melville Herskovits in *Myth of the Negro Past*:

> In the process of conquest which accompanied the spread of the Dahomean kingdom ... the intransigeance of the priests of the river cult was so marked that more than any other group of holy men, they were sold into slavery to rid the conquerors of troublesome leaders. In all those parts of the New World where African religious beliefs have persisted, moreover, the river cult or, in broader terms, the cult of water spirits, holds an important place.
>
> *(Herskovits, 1990, p. 232)*

It was these same holy men who traveled to South America, the Caribbean, and eventually the southern United States. Their influence can be seen in current Vodun and Santeria practices. The "river cults," as they were identified by non-Africanists, participated in sacred water rituals in order to obtain the healing and psychic energy of a named or followed god or ancestor. The immersion into water by Africanist people was to induce the visit of the gods.

This taking over of ego consciousness caused the excitement that we can note in present day spiritual and religious rituals. They include "speaking in tongues" and the rhythmic dance of being taken over by the spirit. African American religious practice is noted for its expectation of a baptism, oftentimes full-body, which mimics the collective spiritual practices of Africanist groups. Melville Herskovits says,

> Among the Ashanti, pilgrimages to Lake Bosumtwe and other sacred bodies of water regularly occur. It is on such occasions that the spirit of the river or lake or sea manifests itself, by "entering the head" of the devotees and causing him to fling himself, possessed, into the water.
>
> *(Herskovits, 1990, p. 233)*

The exchange of energies, that relationship of analysand unconscious to analyst unconscious, has been present in the healing work between "doctor" and patient for centuries. The equality and nature of the work began on the African continent in Egypt as well as African countries below the equator. The model for psychological work between two individuals did not first begin with psychoanalysis but rather had its beginning centuries before in Africa.

The accompanying part of the Transference is the analyst's reaction to what is occurring in the work—how am I affected by what is happening in the transferential relationship. I am not immune to what my patients are feeling. I am expected to be with them in the process in as many ways as possible. We are perhaps engaged in a *participation mystique* connection, but I do not consider it to be some part of a *primitive* "taking over" of consciousness—it is not pathological.

This term, taken from Lévy-Bruhl and used by Jung in a pejorative manner to define a particular state of attention, suggests that the Africans who participated in rituals and experiences of possible healing, entering this joining with another, were fused in a negative way, one directed to their lowered states of consciousness.

I would suggest that Africans and those of the African diaspora have been able to maintain a closeness of bond that has served the social needs of African Americans. In addition, I believe that this ability to participate together in the clinical setting on an unconscious level *can* be brought into consciousness, furthering emotional healing. It would be defeating for a process such as transference to be overshadowed by the belief of connectedness to a *primitive* state, therefore implying that the experience of participation mystique is itself a negative one—one that belongs to *primitive* consciousness and is pathological.

In looking at my own countertransference experience in relationship to African American patients, I must acknowledge our common ground—our cultural life bond.

Jung, in creating his "Other," allowed himself the privilege of being *with* his European companions. Even when he notes how he wants to separate from them—as during his trips to Africa—he still remains tied to them through their cultural collective experience. Just because he wishes to disconnect himself from his cultural collective does not mean that he gets to determine that *our* cultural collective experiences—*participation mystique* as one example—is pathological or shouldn't be accepted. The African American collective experience of slavery has created a psychic bond present in the clinical work because it can be like an archetypal possession. We are joined through the trauma of centuries of psychological and physical suffering.

There are times when my patients are experiencing their emotional trauma in our work together that I can feel the years of pain related to our suffering due to slavery.

This is a part of our cultural collective experience and becomes a part of our necessary analytical work.

In my countertransference, I too experience the profound knowing of the absence, the loss of mother through the slavery generations. My memories of Southern life—sitting in the segregated movie theater, drinking from the "Black only" water fountain, feeling unsafe walking past a group of White boy teenagers when I was 10 years old. I have my recollections, and they are all with me in my work with African American patients. I do not throw away my cultural heritage while doing analytical work, and in consideration of the Transference, it is a part of the work in the same way that Jung's cultural heritage was a part of his work with his patients.

In *Black Issues in the Therapeutic Process*, Dr. Isha McKenzie-Mavinga states,

> A black empathic approach organizes and links the experience of internalized imagery and negative imagination and places it in the context of real lives. To achieve this, the therapist's early experiences of oppression on the basis of skin colour, hair texture, language and case must be processed in the context of his or her exposure to white Western influences on his or her life. Within the relationship of therapist and client, these experiences must be taken into account to enable us to explore how we feel about each other.
>
> *(McKenzie-Mavinga, 2009, p. 71)*

African American dreamwork and cultural consciousness

Jung spent a great part of his life studying and analyzing dreams. We are continuing to learn more about what he already knew—cultural consciousness—but did not put into practice with Africanist dreams. Dreams and the analysis of them give us a wonderful opportunity to allow for a joining of ego and unconscious in promoting a rich, engaging, and meaningful life.

Dreams have been studied since before the days of Egyptian priests and pharaohs. Dreaming was one of the most significant elements of ancient life on the African continent. African cultures have had a rich life of dreaming, understanding dream symbols and obtaining divination directions for how to create authentic lives from their dreams.

In *The African Unconscious: Roots of Ancient Mysticism and Modern Psychology*, Edward Bynum, in his discussion of dreaming and the movement of the African diaspora into the Americas from Asia 36,000 years ago, says the following:

> Continuing the early work of the American Harold Sterling Gladwin in his book *Men out of Asia* (1947), Rinoco Rashidi (1985) and others outline that there was not one, but at least four separate waves of movement into the Americas from Asia. The first to arrive were the Australoids approximately 50,000 to 60,000 years ago. They must have brought with them the seeds of the dreamtime religion and worldviews, a paradigm of dream consciousness as a real state—that dreaming is an entry into an objective condition where contact with ancestors, with forces of animate nature, and where wider biospiritual interactions with the environment are dynamic and possible. Survival technologies emerges from this, such as the so-called "dream travel" and effective medicinal remedies of a practical kind.
>
> *(Bynum, 2012, p. 15)*

The following dream study is from *The Dreams of African American Women: A Heuristic Study of Dream Imagery* (Brewster, 2003). It discusses the dreamer interpretation of one participant's dreams and the symbols that appear in her dreams. Rae is the dreamer whose dreams are presented in this section. A Yoruba *babalawo* shares his interpretations of the dreams. The inclusion of this writing is an opportunity to examine at closer range the dreams and dream symbols of African American women.

In comparing interpretations of several of Rae's dreams from Jungian and Yoruba perspectives, differences did occur regarding interpretation. I believe this is due to cultural differences. The Yoruba tradition has a long history in terms of dream interpretation. Dream interpretation is considered to be a part of the lineage commencing with Esu, the diviner god. Divination is considered a sacred art form by the Yoruba, used to help humans remember their spiritual and psychological tasks in life. The belief is that prior to birth we knew who and what our purpose was on the earth; that, in fact, we have chosen a particular life.

At birth, we forget this purpose, but with the constant help of divination, we are able to understand our life's purpose. Dreams are considered to be within the realm of Esu. When diviners conduct divination readings and do dream interpretation, Esu is the spiritual being they consult for guidance in providing the best interpretation of Ese Ifa. The written poems (*odu*) that tell the diviner what the dreamer needs to know are all contained in Ese Ifa.

The diviner listens to the questions of the dreamer, hears descriptions of the dreams, and provides interpretations based on the dreamer's life circumstance and what Ifa shows in *odu*. The dreamer is able to contribute or retract any information she believes is not accurate during this time with the diviner.

The basis of dream interpretation in Yoruba is spiritual. Jungian dream interpretation has as its basis symbols of Christianity. One of the criticisms made about Jung was his reliance on the Christian "myth" for the development of his psychology theories. In some regards, Jungian psychology is also spiritual because of its reliance on Judeo–Christian symbology.

The following is a description of three of Rae's dreams based on Yoruba, a traditional African model. Baba Ifa Adetunde is an African lineage *babalawo* in the Yoruba tradition. He provides interpretations for the dreams based on his training and experiences as a *babalawo*.

Rae's initial dream was of riding "on a flying carpet with many people." Baba Ifa Adetunde said that this and most of Rae's dreams are spiritual dreams. This initial dream of a magic carpet speaks of spiritual elevation. Baba Adetunde said that the dream is specific to Sufism. The images of others on the carpet are of the ancestors from that part of the world. He believed that those on the carpet were there to offer support in Rae's spiritual development. He said that they provide her with the comfort of their presence and physical direction. The fact that there is someone there who Rae thinks she has an intimate relationship with and that there are so many others "from the same family" indicates the potential for "great support on her spiritual path."

Baba Adetunde believed that there was no connection between Rae's initial flying dream and her second dream of the night, which involved a young couple who had died. He stated that when we dream, we enter the spiritual world, and dreams may become fragmented. It is not necessary to attempt associations between dreams from the same night, as each dream will have its own message and intention.

The beginning of the second dream of the night opened with these words: "I'm at a church service where a young man and woman are being eulogized. People are looking for something to cover their faces." Baba Adetunde said that "this is the dream of someone who will help a lot of people."

Similar to the above dream with others on the carpet, this dream has imagery that includes many people congregated in a church. The place itself is considered to be spiritual, and Baba Adetunde said that this emphasizes the importance of the dream in providing spiritual direction for the dreamer. The dreamer said next, "I suggest some of the women take off their lace veils and put them over their faces. This is done, and the same white cloth is spread over both their faces." In facilitating the covering of their faces, the dreamer is serving as a priestess. "The placing of cloth is a ritual. It means that they are being protected from death."

Rae's dream continued: "An older woman approaches me with an honorary award. She hands it to me and says there will be a celebration at some later time. This award doesn't seem to have anything to do with the funeral and seems a cause for a different kind of ceremony." Baba Adetunde said of these final dream images that they spoke of the potential for Rae to be a priestess.

In fact, he said that the dream is stating that his is her destiny if she wishes. Being offered an honorary award in this dream, coupled with the other images, shows the highest award—which is to be a spiritual teacher of Ifa.

Baba Adetunde's interpretation of the first dream would differ from the Jungian, not as it relates to the meaning, but to what it indicates for ego and awake state functioning. Flying has to do with inflation. This is both a Jungian and Yoruba interpretation. However, in the former this is considered a "problem" in ego development. The magical aspect of flying indicates a *puer-puella* situation that is not supportive of individuation. However, the Yoruba interpretation indicates that flying places the individual closer to God. In this respect, flying is not a problem but a solution. When the dreamer can take on characteristics, like flying, that relate to spiritual beings, these suggest deeper spiritual development. In this way, a significant difference exists between the two interpretations. However, Edinger in *Ego and Archetype* (1992) identified the circle of inflation and deflation and related it to God—the inflated stated was still considered in a negative light exactly because of the ego's identification with the god image.

Baba Adetunde interpreted Rae's snake dream, which follows:

> I go down into the basement of the house looking for someone; I think it's Linda. I notice there is a snake nearby—it's orange with black stripes. Then I notice there are many snakes crawling all over the dirt floor. They're all about the same size: two feet long, either red or orange with black stripes. I become really afraid when I realize how many there are, and tell the man with me that I'm going to leave and go out of there, back upstairs.

Baba Adetunde said that this was a dream of the *egun*. The *egun* are the ancestors, and he explained that *egun* are present in basements and other places beneath the earth. "In Ifa, we understand that the invisible world of our deceased ancestors combines with the visible world of nature and human culture to form a single organic truth" (Neimark, 1993, p. 21). In interpreting this dream, Baba Adetunde acknowledged the power of the *egun*. The location of the snakes determined how the image of the snakes would be interpreted. He stated that Rae may have to face a "frightening experience sometime in the future" because of what he saw in the dream. He recommended that she offer prayers to her ancestors, seeking guidance. He said that the exact circumstance was unclear to him but would present itself to Rae and at the time she would be able to connect it to this particular dream.

In a Benin dream interpretation manual, it states that to dream of a snake is a "very bad omen." It said that the dreamer should speak with a priest and have prayers said for the family. A part of this interpretation mentions enemies and says that if the dreamer kills the snake, he or she will be victorious over his or her enemies. This interpretation is similar to that of Baba Adetunde's belief that snakes do not necessarily represent "good energy." Baba Adetunde clearly stated that the type of snake, its action in dreams, and its location are important elements in determining meaning when snake images are present.

My purpose in providing an interpretation of Rae's dreams by a priest of the Yoruba tradition is to show that cultural symbols do make a difference in how dreams are interpreted. In its almost complete reliance on European symbology for dream interpretation, there is an inherent negation of those belonging to other cultures.

Feminine imagery

Noticeably absent from the African philosophical literature—with one exception—was the voice of women. Equally present in the dreams of the dream participants were female images. Each woman in the study had an equal number of dreams with female images. This strong presence of the feminine suggests a continued awareness and need for this in our present culture. The female images of the dreamers were at times subjectively known to them. At other times, the women in their dreams were strangers. I had the following dream at the beginning of the research project:

> I'm underground with a few other women. I see a brightly colored double-belly clay pot trimmed with the color red. There are other things I've seen but everything else pales next to this pot. The pot is broken off in one place but is a really nice piece.
>
> I go outside and plan to take the pot, but a man standing nearby sees that I have the pot. I tell him I want it and he says that I cannot have it; it belongs to the site. He says something about money as it relates to the pot—do I or am I willing to pay for it?
>
> Now he has moved to a high tower with another woman standing below (who first reported I had taken the pot). The man insists that I cannot have the pot. I tell him okay, but I hold onto it tight, not intending to let go of it.

This dream reminds me of female desire for recapturing that which was stolen from women in the change to a masculine, patriarchy-dominated consciousness. The pot represents all that is feminine and found in the underground once again coming to light.

In speaking of African myths and culture, Karla Holloway in *Moorings and Metaphors: Figures of Culture and Gender in Black Women's Literature* (1992), said that African Americans cannot retrieve that which has been lost; it is possible only to remember. She believed that in the writing of women such as Alice Walker and Toni Morrison, we are able to see the remembrance of that which is mythological to African Americans. I believe that in the dream, the dreams of women, and specifically within the dreams of African Americans, we can see the remembering of

Africanism and African American culture 41

our myths. In our ability to "recover" rather than "retrieve," African American women are capable of having soulfulness through writing. In looking at African myths, Holloway stated that readers must use caution in reading and accepting the interpretations of these African myths. She stated that this is due to the European influence on the interpretation of many West African myths. She suggested that these interpretations were created to suit Western people's points of view regarding their own society.

All three dreamers from this dream study had dreams that contained important, immediately recognizable symbols. The black bull, the mountain, the tree of life that were in the women's dreams are all images that have developed specific meanings over time. Many cultures have defined meanings specific to their society. The interpretations that have evolved from each society generally reflect the development of the image based on its mythic and ritual remembrances.

The analysis and interpretation of most of the dreams are done with the use of European symbols or symbols of indigenous peoples as translated by Europeans.

Sometimes these are accurate and sometimes not.

The African belief that spirit encompasses all life forms justly reflects how symbolic meaning gets created. However, over time and with cultural influence, symbols acquire new meaning.

Following is one of Rae's dreams:

> I'm sitting with a young boy, age 8–10, pulling off a sponge that has grown to his right upper chest. It is a blue rectangle sponge with a black backing. I take off the sponge but it seems another grows back in its place. I say to the woman (mother?) who sits with us that we should try a homeopathic remedy because it would keep it from growing back. That we had to keep it from growing back—that was the solution rather than treating it (from the outside).

Rae and I together chose dream symbols from the above dream that included the following:

8–10-year-old boy	Homeopathic remedy
Sponge	Inside/outside
Blue	Women
Upper right chest	Black

In providing personal associations, Rae identified a feeling of "creepiness" at the idea of the sponge growing on the boy's chest. She said it gave her a "queasy" feeling.

We looked at the purpose of a sponge: what does it do? What was it doing in her dream? Did it change, color, depth, size? How did it feel to the touch? Rae had gone to a homeopathic practitioner for the previous 24 years, ever since the birth of her daughter, so she was familiar with homeopathic medicine. Both the boy and the woman in the dream were unfamiliar. Rae said that, in the dream, she felt concerned and somewhat anxious at the unusualness of the sponge and its ability to keep growing back after several removals.

Baba Adetunde, in looking at the above dream by Rae, saw the image of Olukun, goddess of the ocean. He said that it was a "beautiful" dream.

In *The Way of the Orisha*, Neimark (1993) described Olukun:

> In Africa, Yemonja is represented by the Ogun River rather than by the ocean as she is in the New World. Olukun has come to reflect the bottom or mysterious part of the ocean…. It is here that secrets are preserved and kept, that the unknown is knowable, and that riches and treasures of the world abound.
>
> (p. 118)

According to Baba Adetunde, the dream holds all the energy of the ocean goddess Yemonja or Olukun. The boy is actually one of her children from the sea. The fact that they both appear in Rae's dream highlights her favored status with this goddess. The blue of the sponge is natural to the blue of the ocean. Sponges grow in the ocean. All the dream elements indicated to Baba Adetunde the presence of Olukun and Rae's favored status with this goddess because she is being employed in her service.

In comparison to the interpretation given by Baba Adetunde, the following are possible Jungian interpretations. The sponge soaks up the emotion of the heart *chakra*; there is no flow of passion, it is stopped. The age of the child is that of latency, which is a time for exploring, adventures, and excitement.

However, this child sits quietly and appears to be sad. The sponge is soaking up all of his potential for joy and passion. Lungs become more "spongy" when we are not well—is there some indication of lung-related sickness? The moisture is being held in instead of coming out as it would in a healthy psyche. What is indicated is like with like: a mirroring of sponge with sponge.

Each of these perspectives on the dream offers more information about possible considerations for Rae. This is positive, in that she is able to ascertain her own feelings, beliefs, and associations with both dream interpretations and accept both, one, or neither. If she were to remain only with the images of the dream, perhaps they would take her to the intimacy of Olokun's world. Perhaps, a focus on the sponge as soaking up joy and passion would bring her to the same place. Only the dreamer knows the possibilities because of her lived experience of the dream and its images.

It is possible that a dream will be interpreted in a spiritual light in Yoruba, Jungian, or other frames. On further exploration of the dream, there may emerge possibilities introduced by the dreamer that suggest an archetypal interpretation. Jung was in favor of having a broad-based knowledge of mythology available so that the analyst would have knowledge with which to understand dream images. He felt that this knowledge should come from different fields: mythology, religion, and alchemy. When dreams can be viewed in this kaleidoscopic way, with the dreamer providing guidance, dreams become more meaningful.

In Rae's dream above, one of the identified symbols was the opposite pairing of inside–outside. One of the key features of classical Jungian psychology is identifying symbols within this context of the opposites. It is also a feature that differentiates it from archetypal psychology, wherein a multiplicity of images is supported over a theory of opposites. If opposites come alive as a result of the deepening of imagery, this is fine. However, it is not considered acceptable to have predetermined considerations of opposites before understanding what the image is indicating.

In homeopathy, inside and outside are viewed as reflections of each other. The symptom indicates which remedy is required. When discussing the dream with me, Rae recalled going to the doctor a few months earlier because of a sinus problem. When the homeopathic doctor asked her how she felt, she remembers reporting one of her symptoms as having lungs that felt "spongy." When she received her list of remedies, one of them was a remedy called "sponge." Because of this and other similar experiences, Rae was more readily accepting of the concept of inside and outside as reflections of one another.

Individuation: skin as culture

In the poem *Buckwheat's Lament*, Cornelius Eady writes, "my family tells me this white gang I run with will grow up, and leave me behind…. Wait 'til you're grown…. And I hear this sad place at the middle of that word where they live, where they wait for my skin to go sour."

The cultural consciousness of the African American psychoanalytical client brings a strong identity but one that can be confused and despairing about the very things that make up cultural consciousness. In the above poem by Eady, taken from his book of poems entitled *Brutal Imagination*, an almost-mythological child created by American racial consciousness hears how his skin color will eventually affect him.

Skin color has been an element of importance not only amongst Whites but also amongst Blacks. Perhaps this was so before Africans arrived on American shores. The blackness of the African skin was a mark of beauty or was not based on other aspects of a person's life. There was no comparison to some "other" that qualified it for value.

In *The Color Complex: The Politics of Skin Color Among African Americans*, authors Russell, Wilson, and Hall (1992) say, "A child's awareness and appreciation of the value of different skin colors occurs some time after racial awareness has developed. Some psychologists believe that Black children rarely use skin color as a criterion for racial grouping, but instead rely on facial features, eye color, and hair texture as indicators of Blackness" (p. 65). This is an interesting confirmation of the poet's words in *Buckwheat's Lament* because it is the adults who bring color consciousness. This can sometimes be in service of developing protection against racial violence as one grows into adulthood.

Jung says that Africanist people are, for the most part, unable to individuate. He says that we do not have the level of consciousness necessary for such a feat. Though the psychological life process of Individuation has been connected through writings about rites of passage, once again the *primitive* is not capable of engaging in such a life experience as Individuation because he is non-White. Jung does say however that a few could be capable of individuating but that as a whole, as a group Africanist people are incapable. In taking this idea and deconstructing it I wish to say that Africanist people are individuals, can individuate *and* be a part of a collective. It is once again ironic that the very fact of racism has demanded that African Americans stay true to their individual selves, as well as be participants in their cultural collective for their basic survival—for hundreds of racism-inspired years.

I believe that the initiation rites of passage that Africans have participated in for their entire lives can be considered a mark of individuation for African Americans.

During the course of being initiated, it is usual to receive a tattoo or cut on the skin signifying a new birth or emergence into another social level within the clan. Due to the significance of skin color in American society, perhaps, we are initiated by the mere fact of our skin. We no longer require the markings that set us apart by tribe or village. We now have recognition of this separation by our skin color. But even this takes a while: "By the time they enter elementary school most children have learned to recognize certain subtleties of racial identity. Even so, some stumble over the world 'Black'. To young children, 'black' is foremost a color, not an abstract racial category—and to be told that they are Black when they can see for themselves that they are not can be quite puzzling" (p. 65).

Jung and others since him have taken the ideas of initiation and rites of passage and used them as psychological markers within the clinical work of Jungian psychology. The idea of using individuation as an indication of the ongoing life transformation for African Americans due to skin color is not far-fetched. Our skin has become a marking of many things—both racist and non-racist. If we accept this, which I believe most African Americans do, then we might also accept that we live within the bounds of our skin in a constant rite—a test of transformation as well as survival. This is the course of individuation—a life's work that never ends until mortality comes to the body at the end of this life.

Once we can accept the idea of individuation as a way of life, and knowing that the color of our skin speaks to our culture and determines aspects of how we will live, it seems natural to see how we individuate not only on other factors that might be presented—a divorce, a professional calling, raising children; these and more important markings of life. It also becomes obvious that, for better or worse, our skin color is a marking that supports or denies our ability to individuate. It is a marking of our tribe and our culture and of how we will come to face and engage with our personal life and, in the end, with the collective.

In the psychological world of the beginning years of life, African American children only know the love or hatred that exists in their families. We come of age invited into the home life of parents, grandparents, aunts, and uncles—who are usually excited about receiving us as a new family member.

When the identification is strong with the parents, the music, the rhythm of African American life, then this child can be and will be strong as she or he enters the larger, socialized world of education. Sometimes, it is at this point that children begin to understand the full meaning of skin color. Sometimes, they have already been exposed to the painful reality of what it means to have black skin. This is usually because an adult family member has been emotionally hurt by a racist comment or physically violated in a racist incident. Children overhear these adult conversations and usually begin to ask questions regarding race.

At this point, they may not even know exactly what they are asking about, but the energetic charge that develops when the African American family encounters racism sets the emotions and language on fire. The child feels this heat.

What is not learned within the family at an early age regarding one's skin color is learned within the early experiences at preschool or in kindergarten. Skin color is the most obvious way we can begin to project something of ourselves onto the Other.

It is also the way in which we can begin considering what is important to our cultural conscious. We recognize ourselves because we have learned through our senses regarding that which *belongs* to us as a cultural group. Of course, prior to this we have learned to whom we belong because of our attachment to our mother.

In the larger context of the cultural group, we can sense through smell, touch, sounds, and vision how we fit with our own group. For the most part, this is psychologically comfortable and comforting, like our skin. Then, as children, we begin to hear the dissonance and disconnection that exist based on race. The initial comfort that we experienced in our family of origin begins to break down. This could be one of the first psychological fragmentations within the child. Now we sometimes with warning, and sometimes without, gain what some children and their parents recognize as the trauma of seeing one's skin color again—but this time within the context of race. This often-startling revelation never ceases to be traumatic for the young child. If it is not apparent at the first or second telling, it will become more obvious as the child ages.

There is no African American child who comes of age in America who is left innocent to the possible effects of racism. They must be prepared for the best as well as the worst of what they will encounter as adults of color in America.

This double-sided psychological life is a bind that African American children experience growing up. It is not the *ordinary* life of the typical raising-up where we know life throws us off-guard, presents us with unexpected challenges to our emotional well-being. The *extraordinary* aspect of the African American child's life will be the ability to at first grow into and then bear with, like psychological chains, the existence of American racism. This is the lesson each parent is obligated to teach their children of color. This is the sadness they share, which becomes an intergenerational sorrow.

When Jung spoke of the desire of the "Negro" to exchange his skin for that of the White man, we can see a knowingness on his part of the despair that rested with African Americans during that time, and which is possible even now, as we continue to deal with racist acts of violence against African Americans. What is not obvious in this comment by Jung is at least a show of *empathy* on his part.

This same level of distress that Jung recognized continues to be with African Americans today. There is no way to shake loose the skin. There is no way to become different, because skin is the mark of recognition that brings joy as well as sorrow in the same way as individuation.

This duality of lifelong potential emotional pathos remains as if right under the skin. The possibilities of incidents of racism are also just as close, creating a certain anxiety and vulnerability to being in one's skin while living in the American collective. Some consider this to be one of the results of slavery that is still present with African Americans and labeled under post-traumatic stress disorder.

When the African American client arrives for psychoanalysis this is the sorrow of generations that arrives with them—there is no way to leave it outside the door. There is no desire or wish to leave it outside. It belongs in the room with all the rest of suffering that wants to be healed. The lifetime experience of carrying the skin of color has been impactful in the psychology of the client.

The sourness of skin—touching the American racist collective—causes an *infection* that also requires a remedy, healing. This does not appear to be often acknowledged amongst White American Jungian analysts. The lack of acknowledgment could only add to the further suffering of an African American client. In a life where racism is such a dominant factor, the psychological pain carried by African Americans is tremendous. Jung's *infection* that he speaks about is not *our* infection. African Americans are not the cause of some racial infection given to Whites because of our lower level of consciousness, lack of intelligence, or pre-logical thinking. Racism itself is the infection.

A part of the American collective's racial Shadow is to continually claim amnesia regarding how racism has harmed African Americans. It takes a willingness for the collective, whether that of Jungian psychology or of the general American collective, to also claim that this desire for forgetfulness covers a reluctance to put forth an offering that asks for and invites forgiveness.

This possible repair of what was psychologically traumatizing to African Americans must first begin with the acceptance of how African Americans were harmed by the racism that is embedded in Jung's early statements and writings regarding them. It has not proved sufficient to say only that Jung was just "a man of his times." This phrase has been repeated over several decades and seems to remain ineffective.

Even if this was true, and of course there is some truth to this oft-repeated statement, why is the American Jungian psychology community basically silent on the issue of race and racism within the American collective?

The reluctance to engage with racial issues, historical and contemporary, looks like an attempt to keep racism shadowed—as if it did not exist in Jung's time and does not exist now. In American society, one's skin color speaks whether we want this or not. We assume a certain knowledge, projections of one another, because of skin color. Even when we do not physically touch, we still touch one another. We are psychically connected through centuries of archetypal DNA. How relevant or important is this fact to our psychoanalytical work? At some point in the work, as in life, race—all of its constructed elements and issues related to racism emerge.

This is true because the client needs to release the psychological burden of being *that* skin color with all its accompanying painful weight, as does the analyst, whether White or Black. This aspect of existence must be discussed, reconciled, and accepted within cultural contexts for both analyst and analysand.

There is oftentimes a refusal on the part of the client to accept that the American collective of Shadow can still persist; can still affect his or her life. The initial trauma returns, as do the other personal traumas experienced at an earlier age, causing disbelief and horror at how one's skin is creating a life—unconsciously in many cases.

This is not because the client does not know that racism or racial problems exist but because the racial complexes and the Shadow holding the amnesia of racial forgetfulness conspire to keep the pain of the psychological confines of skin color buried in the personal Shadow.

It is through memory that we know who we are. This constant exposure to the feel of our skin matters in remaining connected to our bodies and our minds. This connection determines our good all-round health. The skin in which we were born belongs to us and we belong to it. The psychological exposure felt at being African American at times grips the skin called one's own. During this time, there seems to be little we can do about this grip because racism does exist; we bear our skin exposing it to life. Such a strong archetypal energy as racism requires individual reflection, as well as a willingness for self-reflection, on the part of groups within the larger American collective.

Considerations of our skin color, and all that is significant about it, are reflected in the collective American psyche. This is not the problem. The racism that hides in the Shadow of this collective psyche continues to be the psychological challenge for each member of American society, including American Jungians. My skin reflects a process of initiation, a hard-fought and difficult rite of passage that I must often endure under a variety of life trials for *all* of my life. Individuation is the same.

Surviving through slavery and post-slavery into contemporary times, my ancestors and all who followed them knew what it was to individuate. Meanwhile, they remained bound to our cultural collective. Our skin is a mark of our ability to individuate as well as to be survivors within our cultural heritage. The work is to consider these Jungian theoretical concepts such as individuation, transference, and dreamwork; to re-collect them and show their place of origin with a sense of honor.

The task is to individuate beyond any preconceived negative racial idea regarding the invented limitations of skin color, claiming what rightfully belongs to a life, no matter the color of skin.

References

Alexander, Michelle. (2012). *The New Jim Crow: Mass Incarceration in the Age of Colorblindness*. New York: The New Press.

Brewster, Fanny. (2011). *The Dreams of African American Women: A Heuristic Study of Dream Imagery*. Ann Arbor, MI: Pro Quest UMI Dissertation Publishing.

Brewster, Fanny. (2016). "Journey: The Middle Passage, Poems" (forthcoming). *Psychological Perspectives Journal*. London: Taylor and Francis.

Bynum, Edward Bruce. (2012). *The African Unconscious: Roots of Ancient Mysticism and Modern Psychology*. New York: Cosimo Books.

Eady, Cornelius. (2001). *Brutal Imagination*. New York: Putnam.

Edinger, E. (1992). *Ego and Archetype: Individuation and the Religious Function of the Psyche*. Boston, MA, and London: Shambhala Publications.

Herskovits, Melville J. (1990). *The Myth of the Negro Past*. Boston, MA: Beacon Press.

Holloway, K. (1992). *Moorings and Metaphors: Figures of Culture and Gender in Black Women's Literature*. New Brunswick, NJ: Rutgers University Press.

James, George G. M. (1992). *Stolen Legacy: Greek Philosophy Is Stolen Egyptian Philosophy*. Trenton, NJ: Africa World Press, Inc.

Jung, C. G. (1954/1970). *The Practice of Psychotherapy*. CW 16.

Lawson, Thomas E. (1984). *Religions of Africa: Traditions in Transformation*. San Francisco: Harper and Row Publishers.

Lévy-Bruhl, L. (1960). *How Natives Think*. New York: Washington Square Press.

Mbiti, John. (1989). *African Religions and Philosophy* (2nd ed.). Portsmouth, NH: Heinemann Publishers.

McKenzie-Mavinga, Isha. (2009). *Black Issues in the Therapeutic Process*. London: Palgrave Macmillan.

Neimark, P. (1993). *The Way of the Orisha: Empowering Your Life Through the Ancient African Religion of Ifa*. New York: HarperCollins Publishers.

Russell, K., M. Wilson, and R. Hall. (1992). *The Color Complex: The Politics of Skin Color Among African Americans*. New York: Doubleday.

Tough, Paul. (2009). *Whatever It Takes: Geoffrey Canada's Quest to Change Harlem and America*. Boston, MA: Houghton Mifflin Harcourt.

5
AFRICAN ARCHETYPAL PRIMORDIAL
A map for Jungian Psychology

Cape Coast Castle

A man stumbles
into the dark hole of this space
several more follow
they too fall,
feces dust rise to their mouths
to their eyes,
they are bound close
unable to see beyond the march
from forest to ocean

In this room the air bends back
folding into itself
their fever-coughs
bounce from sweating stones
and collapse on over-burdened ears

The river water flows free under their dungeon
mindful of them
but unable to stop its motion
the men listen,
to wave after wave
beating stone,
their voices cry to be heard

but being free
smelling their forest scent

> without memory of them as children
> only the river speaks,
> and their voices fall silent
>
> Fanny Brewster
Journey: The Middle Passage

One of the most psychologically difficult aspects of African American contemporary life continues to be the "sense" of a lack of history due to the systematic attempts to eradicate or malign African history, inclusive of every aspect of its culture. Ironically enough, Jungian psychology holds several elements of what I consider as deriving from African psychological and archetypal maps. This intention to discredit and, in many cases, to destroy this history (while making use of African cultural models) has occurred across every aspect of American society, including within the field of psychology. The period of time within the field of American psychology that epitomizes the most racist view of African Americans was most vehemently expressed through *eugenics*.

In *Even the Rat Was White: A Historical View of Psychology*, author Robert Guthrie gives the reader a look at the beginning of the use of "science" to establish the "facts" regarding the lesser intelligence of African Americans:

> The earliest recorded attempt by American researchers to measure psychological capacities in different races was made in 1881 when C.S. Meyers tested Japanese subjects and proved that the Asians were slower in reaction time than Europeans. Shortly afterwards, utilizing a popular reaction time device, Bache (1895) tested American Indians and Blacks and concluded that these "primitive peoples" were highly developed in physiological tests and attributes while "higher" human forms "tended less to quickness of response in the automatic sphere; *the reflective man is the slower being.*"
>
> (Guthrie, 2004, p. 47, italics added)

Guthrie states, "As late as 1973, Henry Garrett, a past president of the American Psychological Association, supported this theory (of skull size designating intellectual capacity) when he wrote that the Black man's brain 'on the average is smaller ... less fissured and less complex than the white brain.'"

These "scholarly" ideas regarding African Americans initially began through the anthropological work of men "exploring" Africa. The justification for slavery and later religious conversion of Africans was partially substantiated by discrediting Africans by skull size and other physical limitations.

When we look to African culture, developed from a variety of African countries, we see areas of richness including art, dance, philosophy, religion, and psychology.

Oftentimes, the art of psychology was based on traditional healing practices.

M. Vera Buhrman, a Jungian analyst and author of *Living in Two Worlds: Communication between a White Healer and Her Black Counterparts* (1986), became a practitioner of Xhosa medicine through her training with Mongezi Tiso.

The Tiso School, where Buhrmann studied for nine years, is useful in giving us an understanding of African medicine specific to psychological healing. This is especially important due to its close connectedness, philosophically, to the underpinnings of belief that support Jungian psychological theories. Buhrmann expresses a belief that Xhosa medicine was based on Jungian concepts of psychology.

I would differ with her in this, suggesting rather that depth psychology, as developed by Jung, was oftentimes based in part on the social and spiritual concepts of indigenous people, including Africans.

Buhrmann states:

> In my work the world-view of the Nguni people is relevant, especially as it pertains to mental health and ill-health, i.e. the psychological aspect in its widest sense. It is important to make the latter point, because Western medicine divides illness into the different categories of somatic, psychological and psychosomatic; the Black people do not: they say that "when part of me is ill, the whole of me is ill", irrespective of what the illness is.
>
> (Buhrmann, 1986, p. 26)

Due to the fact that we are considering the art of psychology, other areas of African culture will not be discussed in great detail in this chapter. The focus is on the lineage of healing within the scope of psychology that shows lines of connection between the cultural aspects of traditional African healing practices and their potentiality for African American psychological healing.

Another important source of information regarding African healing practices, comes from John Janzen, who, like Buhrman—but unlike Jung and Freud—spent time actually researching African healing communities. His text, *Ngoma: Discourses in Healing in Central and Southern Africa* (1992), provides detailed descriptions of medicine as practiced among these communities.

These communities, given the English name "cults of affliction" by Victor Turner, provided not only psychological support for individuals but also a social and cultural context within which healing could occur. The word *ngoma*, which means drum, is relevant as drumming and dance were vital components of the healing rituals for community members requiring medicinal support.

Of significance is the emphasis on the involvement of family and community in a healing ritual that was led by a traditional healer.

Janzen gives the reader a detailed description of his experiences of meeting with healers, including the following:

> In the city of Kinshasa, he met with a healer who was of the *nkita* lineage. Nkita defined not only the lineage, but also the name of the illness, the spirit behind the illness, and the therapeutic rite to be performed for healing. Janzen spoke of the signs of affliction particular to the patients seeing this healer: psychological distress, disturbing dreams, fever, childhood disease, and female infertility. The patient's illnesses became areas of specialty for the healer. The initial healing ceremony took place at a river.
>
> (Brewster, 2011, p. 123)

This experience as described by Janzen reminds me of how in archetypal psychology, the god that appears has a particular "affliction" as well as the remedy for healing. It is important to note that Jung did make a trip to Central Africa in 1925, which he describes in *Memories, Dreams, Reflections*. However, he did not stay for any extensive studies with African individuals or communities. In fact, his visit, as he himself described it, was one of fear. He had left Europe concerned about his psychological state, hoping to visit Africa and get relief. While in Africa, he describes his fear of "going black" and losing his European consciousness. His anxiety was about falling into a more "primitive," *lower state* of consciousness. This appears to have been an immense anxiety for Jung at different times in his life, not only in relationship to becoming *victim* to an African consciousness.

An important aspect of the ngoma is that those who become healers of this tradition experience a sickness or illness suggestive of a psycho-spiritual calling.

This is suggestive of the same way in which Jungian analysts are brought into their profession, as handmaidens of the soul. Sometimes, an illness appearing within a dream, or in the body, is indicative of ngoma, a spiritual calling to become a healer.

It would appear that many Jungian analysts consider their work to be a call by spirit—Jung might say, a *spirit of the depths*, to enter into the spiritual work of psychoanalysis. Jung, at one point in expressing his own calling in *The Red Book*, says, "the spirit of the depths was silent in me, since I swayed between fear, defiance, and nausea, and was wholly the prey of my passion. I could not and did not want to listen to the depths. But on the seventh night, the spirit of the depths spoke to me: 'Look into your depths, pray to your depths, waken the dead'" (2009, p. 140).

Until very recent times, within the past two decades, African Americans have been extremely reluctant to engage in formal psychotherapeutic practice as patients.

Practitioners have given varying reasons for this lack of engagement by people of color. One reason that seems apparent is the lack of trust, dating from the early days of psychoanalysis, between the founding members of psychoanalysis and African Americans.

In their book *Psychotherapy with African American Women: Innovations in Psychodynamic Perspectives and Practice*, practicing therapists Leslie Jackson and Beverly Greene list nine basic reasons why African American women might be reluctant to engage in psychodynamic therapy.

The focus of early psychoanalysis was on *needing* patients who were "crazy."

There was a very large stigma placed on anyone who required being seen by a medical doctor for psychological or emotional treatment. The authors list this as one of the major reasons the women with whom they worked would not want psychotherapy.

It was not unusual for African Americans in those early days of the twentieth century, as is often the case now, to receive a lesser standard of healthcare as compared to Whites. Economics and race were generally significant in whether or not an individual could be taken care of by the medical profession.

In American society from the early days of slavery, Africans were not initially allowed to be taught how to read English; then, later, schools could not be built for them and finally, when these schools were built, African Americans were segregated into the worst schools possible based on Jim Crow laws. Colleges did not readily accept African American men or women as doctoral students. Francis Cecil Sumner was the first such graduate in 1920 under the mentoring of Stanley Hall. He completed a doctoral thesis on Freud and Adler. The first African American woman to complete her doctoral degree was Inez Beverly Prosser in 1933. It was in Educational Psychology.

The number of applicants for graduate programs was extremely limited and enrollment was discouraged. Under these conditions, it was unlikely that a formally trained psychoanalyst would be available for African Americans, in cities or particularly in rural areas. Dr. Sumner attempted to remedy this situation as one of the founders of Howard University's Psychology Department.

Africanist cultural tradition indicates medicine was a communal experience that was heavily dependent not only on one individual in a private setting but also on family and extended family members. It was vital to know what was considered "sickness" and what was "normal" for the *culture*. Psychoanalysis, particularly in its early years, would not have been positively responsive to African Americans, except in the most extreme cases where hospitalization was a factor, such as in Jung's case with St. Elizabeth Hospital. Even then, the treatment may have taken the form of a physiological experiment, though William Alanson White was working at changing the American model of psychology from one of laboratory-focused research experiments to psychoanalysis. Meanwhile, the families of mentally ill patients strived to take care of them at home without the intervention of "outsiders"—psychiatric medical doctors.

The medical establishment that African Americans encountered from their very earliest days in America, including psychiatric care, was in many ways reminiscent of those European doctors who gradually over time began to replace the traditional African healers. However, along with this newer relationship, perhaps, came the mistrust of removing the process of healing patients away from cultural norms with its focus on body–mind connection, dreams, family involvement, and respect for ancestors as a part of understanding mental sickness and its remedy. Is the contemporary mistrust of African Americans a continued underlying effect of early psychoanalysis, which even today can negatively impact patient–doctor relations? How do the long-standing cultural aspects of African traditional healing practices, discounted by European *civilized* medical principles and practice, remain stifled in African Americans many generations later?

One significant aspect of African healing points to the Jungian archetypal idea that the gods cause our psychological "illness" and that this selective god who has brought the sickness also holds the remedy for our psychological healing. In this view, a healing at the deepest level—soulfulness—is expected.

This appears strongly related to Xhosa beliefs that the ancestors were an important part of a patient's ability to heal. Dreams represented the way in which a patient could understand her illness and also the manner in which the sickness could be treated or cured. In Xhosa culture, the ancestors were believed to have communicated through dreams. Jung's idea was that the archetypal gods communicated to us through our dreams. Asclepius and others in working with dreams invited the dreamer into a space where dream and healing took place almost simultaneously.

A supportive environment was essential and this included a great deal of *trust*.

Perhaps, this level of trust cannot yet be established in patients of color as regards psychoanalysis due to the African experience of colonialism and the African American experience of slavery, psychoanalysis's medical treatment of African Americans, and its accompanying racism toward patients as well as those training to become medical doctors. In *Living with Racism: The Black Middle-Class Experience*, authors Feagin and Sikes provide the following insight taken from an African American: "Black medical professionals with whom we talked often reported having a difficult time in school or in the early years of practice, in that they were tested in unfair ways or were expected to fail" (1994, p.116).

John Janzen stated that his text *Ngoma: Discourses in Healing in Central and Southern Africa* (1992) was an attempt to create a more popularly acceptable concept and view of the healing communities, or ngoma cults, that existed in southern and central Africa. These communities, named "cults of affliction" by anthropologist Victor Turner, were distinguished in African communities not only for their therapeutic effect but also as socializing elements.

They provided support and emotional comfort in times of physical and psychological difficulty. *Ngoma*, defined as "drum," signified the presence of drumming and dancing in the ritualistic ceremonies conducted under the direction of a traditional healer. Janzen provided a detailed and rich written report of the nuances of the ngoma. In doing so, he pointed to the historical and contemporary nature of the ngoma.

Reviewing the current status of medicine in Africa, he strongly suggested that the ngoma be recognized as an established institution. He believed this would greatly support the development of social agencies for the care of sick individuals. He noted that ngomas thrive in African communities and should be supported in a broad manner for the social, psychological, and physical well-being of Africans.

In his opening chapter, Janzen took the reader to the four geographical areas he selected for his research on the ngoma communities. These comprised Kinshasa (Zaire), Dar es Salaam (Tanzania), Mbabane-Manzini (Swaziland), and Cape Town, South Africa. These areas were chosen because they differ from each other in language and in general social custom.

Janzen detailed his meetings with healers. He described their work with patients and his own personal experience of ngoma work with several of these healers. For example, in the city of Kinshasa, he met with a healer who was of the *nkita* lineage.

Nkita defined not only the lineage, but also the name of the illness, the spirit behind the illness, and the therapeutic rite to be performed for healing. Janzen spoke of the signs of affliction particular to the patients seeing this healer: psychological distress, disturbing dreams, fever, childhood disease, and female infertility. The patients' illnesses became areas of specialty for the healer. The initial healing ceremony took place at a river.

An important element of the ngoma is that, in many respects, it serves as an initiation to become novices and eventually healers within a healing community. The sickness or illness experienced by individuals is often considered to be a spiritual calling to become a healer. However, it can also be a sickness brought on by magic or due to disrespect for the ancestors. The nature of the illness and its origin is determined by the healer, who provides guidance about the healing solution.

Another important feature of ngoma is that this tradition, which began in rural areas of Africa, is now common in urban life. Janzen noted that the negative side of this is the dominance of charlatans preying on lonely, sick people who have moved to urban areas due to poverty and stressful circumstances in their homelands. However, he said that the more positive side is the considerable exchange of healing therapies and remedies from a variety of communities whose members have met in urban areas.

In reviewing ngoma on the Swahili coast, Janzen recalled the work of Hans Cory, an ethnologist from the early twentieth century, who recorded the ngoma communities and their makeup.

Cory observed that they were communities not only for ancestor reverence and divination, but also served as guilds for professional and artistic development.

Janzen interviewed Botoli Laie, a healer from this area. Laie noted the spirits that afflict and describe the accompanying sicknesses. Omari, the second healer interviewed, stated that he learned ngoma from his father and was not himself a "sufferer-novice."

Omari was viewed by the author as more of a medical doctor with a clinical practice. However, Omari did work with patients who had *sheitani* (spirit) sickness, and he stated that he referred patients with "ordinary sickness" to the hospital.

In South Africa, Janzen described a different ngoma that he believed was influenced by the hostile and potentially volatile atmosphere of the townships. Within this atmosphere, the ngoma offered a much-needed place of solace and support. The author noted that one of every four households belonged to a ngoma. He described in a case study the initiation of Ntete, a Cape Town man. Janzen compared the differences and similarities in ceremonies between Cape Town and other ngoma locations.

The basic nature of the rituals remained the same as those conducted in the rural countryside: calling the ancestors, smearing medicine on the initiate's body, the sacrifice of a goat, and dancing and singing.

All activities were completed over a three-day period. Janzen observed that this ngoma of Cape Town had several of the main features of the broader ngoma institution. These included the entry of a sick person into ngoma training under the supervision of a healer, novices working together to learn and study dreams, and songs and divination practices. Individuals celebrated rites of passages through sacrifice and the sharing of meals.

Janzen stressed the importance of lexicon in determining the nature of ngoma. He described in detail the origin of ngoma and how this aspect of African life spread from one location to another. He determined that by tracing the linguistic features of the Bantu languages through selected African regions, he could observe the history and development of ngoma. He discussed ngoma musical instruments and how they promoted development of ngoma as an institution. Janzen stated that the methodology of genetic classification has been the key factor in determining the historical development of ngoma through shared features. He provided a list of cognate terms that "reveals symptoms, etiologies, healer roles, medicines and ritual activities with end-goal of health of cognate reconstructions based on a comparison of modern semantic variations" (1992, p. 63). For example, the Bantu proto-cognate word for *dog* suggests that that which causes sickness also heals. Janzen described the core features of ngoma therapy, from the initial sickness and identification by an established healer through the ceremonial rituals of whitening the body, purification ceremonies, and dream and divination training.

Again referring to Turner, Janzen noted the rites of passage in the separation of sacred and profane space and time in the healing rituals.

Divination, a diagnostic tool, is always a part of the work of the ngoma. It assists the healer in determining the cause of the sickness and the direction of the healing.

Spirits are a major feature of ngoma therapy and must be communicated with, either through channeling or through requests for assistance in healing. Often, spirits are identified as the source of the sickness. Someone following this *sign*, indicated by sickness or dreams, will become a healer in the spiritual community or ngoma of this identified spirit. It is believed that a society should remain stable and without *misfortune*. The sacrifices made by the ngoma assure its members of good fortune.

Janzen stated that the animal sacrifice "purifies the universe in that it restores or regenerates the human community to its ideals" (1992, p. 104).

In my opinion, Janzen's recommendation of the ngoma as a recognized institution would be most beneficial to Africans. A social institution that has remained as consistent as this one should be supported. Additionally, the ngoma is a purely African institution that has survived and provided much for the spiritual and financial well-being of Africans. Its ability to withstand the pressures and influences of colonialism proves its viability. Based on Janzen's research, it appears that there are correlations between ngoma healing practices and those of modern medicine.

Bantu Folklore by Matthew Hewat (1970) was originally published in 1906. It has been chosen for inclusion because of the author's apparent familiarity with the social customs of the Bantu people.

According to Hewat, when death came suddenly, it was believed to be caused by family members, and they were the first to be held under suspicion. Within Bantu cosmological belief, a spirit world existed. Sacrifices by "medicine men" were offered to appease the "offended spirits" and were also made when someone dreamed of the ancestors. Hewat described in detail the specific rituals for offering sacrifices. He also reported that amulets were worn by most Bantus as a form of protection against sickness and evil.

Hewat noted that there were several different kinds of *amagqira* (doctors), including herbalists, witch doctors, and surgeons. They could be either men or women. The doctors could attain this position through lineage or choose the path of medicine on their own. Individuals who became doctors or healers went through a training period.

This training began after the initiate was identified as having a calling through a dream, a spirit river calling, and visions. Once these events occurred, then training with a teacher began. Hewat stated, "Taking a herb doctor all-round he is often a clever fellow, good at the cure of some diseases, and his methods and principles compare favourably with those ascribed to Aesculapius and Galen in the early history of medicine" (1970, p. 28).

In Chapter 4, Hewat provided the reader with a list of diseases, causes, and prescribed traditional cures. Chapter 5 continued in the same manner but also included instances where surgery was performed and stated the medicines for diseases where surgery was necessary.

Hewat also wrote about the Bantu rituals related to midwifery and children. Of particular note was the rite carried out 10 days following birth: placing children in a hole in the earth to protect them and keep them healthy. Related and of equal significance was the burial of small children in the earth when they appeared to be getting sick. In his summary, Hewat allowed that native healers or doctors were knowledgeable and adequately prepared to provide healthcare services to their patients.

Harriet Ngubane lived among the Zulu people, conducting anthropological fieldwork. The text *Body and Mind in Zulu Medicine: Ethnography of Health and Disease in Nyuswa-Zulu Thought and Practice* (1977) was a result of her investigative studies. In opening, she said that her book grew out of "a desire to look into social behaviour that was considered traditional" (p. 2). In this introductory section, Ngubane discussed the advantages and disadvantages of being Zulu to completing her research study. Chapter 1 began with a historical review of the Nyuswa people. The Nyuswa, according to Ngubane, had resided on their land for 130 years. They were a clan people with strong lineage lines. She said of them, "I would argue that in spite of Christianity the permeating influence in the Nyuswa reserve is based more on Zulu culture than any foreign culture" (Ngubane, 1977, p. 20).

In Chapter 2, Ngubane discussed the causes of sickness and related facts and defined various terms. *Umuthi* (medicine) is a tree or shrub that is both poisonous and curative. *Isifo* is defined as somatic symptoms, misfortune, or disease. In Zulu culture, illness has two major causes. One is biological (natural forces), which occur as part of the life process—that is, aging, childhood illnesses, seasonal sickness, and family genealogical sickness. This type of illness is termed *umkhuhlane*. Medicines used for umkhuhlane are not part of a ritual but are considered sufficiently potent to help with sickness. Africans believe that non-Africans are capable of understanding these kinds of illnesses but not those "based on Zulu cosmology" (p. 2). *Ukufa kwaban* was defined as a disease of the African peoples. "This name is used mainly because the philosophy of causality is based on African culture" (p. 24).

The second major cause of illness was directly related to an imbalance in the psychic and physical environment of an individual. "Pollution" existed through sorcery or the negative actions of one person or animal upon another. This "pollution" could be reversed by a balancing between order and disorder. "For a Zulu conceives good health not only as consisting of a healthy body, but as a healthy situation of everything that concerns him.... Good health means the harmonious working and coordination of his universe" (Ngubane, 1977, p. 27). There were some who were considered more vulnerable to environmental pollution; those included infants, strangers, and individuals who had been sick for long periods of time without treatment. In the chapter discussing sorcery, Ngubane said that it resulted from intentional pollution of the environment that left something behind that caused illness. According to the author, everyone had the right and was expected to protect himself or herself against sorcery. She listed three types of sorcerers: night sorcerers, day sorcerers, and lineage sorcerers.

Another chapter of Ngubane's text (1977) was devoted to a discussion of ancestors and sickness. Zulu belief is that ancestors are a major factor in health and sickness; the living have a responsibility to respect and acknowledge their ancestors.

When this does not occur, it is more likely that an individual or close family member with "Pollution" was considered to have mystical powers. There were two situations in which it usually dominated. The first was the birth of a child, and the second was death.

Other circumstances considered to be polluted (but less so) were menstruation and the day after sexual intercourse. Someone who murdered another was considered to be in a polluted state. In order to rid oneself of pollution, it was necessary to seek treatment.

This treatment was typically sought from three different sources. Classified by group, these included the diviner, the bone thrower, and whistling great ancestors. Herbal medicine was considered a part of treatment and was classified according to the colors red, black, and white. "Colour plays an important and dominant role in symbolism related to therapy of mystical illness," reported Ngubane (1977, p. 113).

The colors black, red, and white were always used in strict observance of sequence. Black and red were considered equal, both good and bad. White was held to be good. Black and red medicine was always followed by white medicine. The former two were used in treatment to rid the body of what was considered to be bad: the sickness. White was then given in order to restore the individual to good health. The colors were related to the "cosmic order of day and night." It was believed that danger existed at night in the form of night sorcerers, sick people, and ancestral spirits. Black medicine was necessary to help restore health and provide a time for resting. "Herein lies the relevance of the equivocal power of black medicines. While they are dangerous, they are nevertheless necessary to make a person strong and powerful" (Ngubane, 1977, p. 115).

Sunrise and sunset that had a reddish color represented the state between something dark and something light. In discussing red medicines, Ngubane said, "Red compared with black represents less danger and more good" (1977, p. 116). Going further, she added, "Daylight represents life and good health. To be (mystically) ill is likened to moving away from the daylight into the dimness of the sunset and on into the night." In sorcery, it is black medicine that is used, which signifies the darkness, the night. In order for one to become healthy, one must move from night to day. Ngubane also stated that "illness is associated with heat." Black and red medicines were always heated before application. In contrast, white medicines were usually not heated before application. Although the author refers to the theory of color evolution by Berlin and Kay, where colors evolve from stage one (black and white) to stage seven (purple, pink, orange, or gray), she stated that she did not find it relevant in her study of Zulu society.

Once the illness was removed, it was usually placed in one of two locations: either cast onto an animal (a goat or black bull) or at crossroads and on highways. It was hoped that in this secondary way, a passing stranger would absorb and carry the evil away with him. Ngubane wrote that "The symbolic therapy is fixed and standardized for each mystical illness. It is not abandoned if good results are not realized, but is repeated all over again, because such rites are rites of transformation, rites of process, of passage from a mystical state of darkness to one of mystical light. Treatment in this sense is a religious act" (1977, p. 132).

Ngubane carefully outlined in the succeeding chapters the Zulu view of the nature of spirit possession. In the summary conclusion, she discussed spirit possession, anthropology, and its relationship to Zulu beliefs. Referencing Gluckman, Levi-Strauss, and Turner, Ngubane concluded that women were not witches and that sorcery was masculine, pollution feminine. She referenced Turner's symbology of colors: red for transition, white for life, and black as an indication of death. She applied Levi-Strauss's raw-cooked symbology to the Zulu concepts of good and evil opposites.

Ngubane's research and discussion of Zulu healing practices touched on several topics by other authors. The fact that black medicine was found to be so necessary to the healing process is reminiscent of Hillman's insistence on darkness and the journey to the underworld. The *umuthi* (medicine) is both a poison and a curative. Meier (1967) noted the Greek acceptance of this healing concept in his text. Like Ngubane, Meier said it was someone from another world—a god (or ancestor)—who brought sickness. I note the strong similarities between Ngubane's findings related to healing practices and those of others. The longevity of African healing practices suggests a capacity for healing that goes beyond the body-only orientation of modern medicine. It inherently relates directly to that which is spiritual.

In his text *Working with the Dreaming Body* (1985), Arnold Mindell presented 50 case studies. He discussed the relationship between dreams and physical illness. His belief was that body symptoms are mirrored in dreams and vice versa, and that these symptoms intensify as the body seeks health. Mindell related his story of becoming sick and the effect this had on his perspective as he viewed his body's attempts to heal itself. In an example from a patient's life, he tells of a patient dying from a tumor.

The author worked on increasing the level of psychic pain in the stomach, pushing for something to "break through." The patient had never been able to communicate with others in a manner he found satisfactory. Mindell believed that because of their work together, the patient reached a point where he was able to successfully express himself.

The patient was relieved of his painful stomach symptoms and survived longer than expected.

I believe that Mindell's approach to dreamwork, with its emphasis on body healing, mirrors the African system of healing's inclusiveness of body and mind in the process. In Jung's theory, there is recognition of the place of consciousness working with the unconscious. I interpret his use of the word "conscious" within this context as an awareness that is inclusive of the body as part of ego functioning.

Amplification is the process Mindell used in his work with patients to discover the "channel" through which the body was attempting to manifest symptoms. He amplified both the dream experience and the body or proprioceptive experience.

Mindell (1985, p. 9) described his work as process work, stating that it is a "natural science.... I simply look to see what exactly is happening in the other person and what happens to me while he is reacting." He did not credit himself or the therapist with any special skill but rather stated, "The therapist's only tool is his ability to observe processes. He has no pre-established tricks or routines." It is through this process that the next actions can be predicted.

Mindell proceeded further to define *process*. He noted that the term is not viewed from a psychological perspective but rather from that of a physicist. He said of process that the primary feature is being close to awareness of all that is transpiring.

Additional features include identifying "unconscious" body symptoms, working without judgment, and the use of neutral language in exchanges with patients.

Mindell said (1985, p. 13), "I don't believe the person actually creates disease, but that his soul is expressing an important message to him through the disease." He supported this statement by relating how many of his patients—most of whom were dying—moved from just being sick to a life-affirming process of inner development. He stated that often these patients were initially not interested in analysis, only in physical healing. An example he provided was of a woman, Frau Herman, who had cancer. In what Mindell considered a dream related to her physical condition, she took a trip to the gym. Later, she dreamed of a woman with milk in her breast. Mindell believed this dream opened her consciousness to being cured of cancer. Through the dream series of this patient, Mindell was able to follow the path of physical healing from beginning to end. "The body has many centers and points of awareness. Your body uses projections and psychological problems to stimulate discovery of its different parts" (Mindell, 1985, p. 31).

Mindell said that shamans knew and understood about projection as a cause of illness by the placing of "black magic" on another. He believed that projections could make one sick.

He told of a man with goiter, a throat problem, who had a very difficult and controlling father. As the patient was able to become physical, punching and hitting and screaming his hate for his father, he was physically and mentally released from negative father projections. Mindell maintained that the withdrawing of the negative projection from the father and the acceptance of his feelings of hatred enabled the patient to heal. He stated that successful bodywork depends entirely on the patient.

Mindell believed that the dreambody is a multichanneled personality. He noted the process of healing changes "channels" and goes from hearing to feeling, feeling to visualizing, and from seeing to moving. He indicated that it is through the experience of feeling pain that one is awakened to consciousness. When the pain becomes too intense, one changes channels and moves toward health. Mindell said the dreambody signals to the physical body, identifying a symptom. The ability to switch from one channel to another in the process, Mindell believed, is often a matter of life and death. If one cannot move in the direction of healing, then one dies, remaining, in effect, stuck in one channel.

Mindell reviewed the dreambody in fairy tales and couple relationships and as a part of the world collective. He believed that understanding oneself makes for a better understanding of the world collective dreambody. Mindell stated that at an early age, one might discover illnesses that would be chronic because they usually appeared in childhood dreams. He outlined a plan for working alone, without an analyst, with the dreambody, using increased awareness, amplification, and channel-changing as phases in the process.

Mindell concluded his text by indicating that dying individuals beginning dreambody work often feel that they are getting better and report feeling less sick. Mindell summarized that this is because the dreambody is containing and healing the physical body even as it approaches death.

References

Brewster, Fanny. (2011). *The Dreams of African American Women: A Heuristic Study of Dream Imagery*. Ann Arbor, MI: Pro Quest UMI Dissertation Publishing.

Brewster, Fanny. (2016). "Journey: The Middle Passage, Poems" (forthcoming). *Psychological Perspectives Journal*. London: Taylor and Francis.

Buhrmann, M, Vera. (1986). *Living in Two Worlds: Communication Between a White Healer and Her Black Counterparts*. Wilmette, IL: Chiron.

Feagin, Joe R. and Melvin P. Sikes. (1994). *Living with Racism: The Black Middle-Class Experience*. Boston, MA: Beacon Press.

Greene, Beverly and Leslie C. Jackson. (2000). *Psychotherapy with African American Women: Innovations in Psychodynamic Perspectives and Practice*. New York: Guilford Press.

Guthrie, R. (2004). *Even the Rat Was White: A Historical View of Psychology*. Boston, MA: Pearson Education.

Hewat, Matthew. (1970). *Bantu Folklore*. Westport, CT: Negro University Press.

Hillman, James. (1979). *The Dream and the Underworld*. New York: Harper and Row.

Janzen, J. (1992). *Ngoma: Discourses in Healing in Central and Southern Africa*. Berkeley, CA: University of California Press.

Jung, C. G. (1993). *Memories, Dreams, Reflections* (13th ed.). New York: Random House.
Jung, C. G. (2009). *The Red Book: Liber Novus*. New York: W.W. Norton.
Meier, C. A. (1967). *Healing Dream and Ritual: Ancient Incubation and Modern Psychotherapy*. Einsiedeln, Switzerland: Daimon Verlag.
Mindell, A. (1985). *Working with the Dreaming Body*. London: Penguin Books.
Ngubane, H. (1977). *Body and Mind in Zulu Medicine: Ethnography of Health and Disease in Nyuswa-Zulu Thought and Practice*. London and New York: Academic Press.
Turner, Victor. (1993). *Drums of Affliction: A Study of Religious Processes among the Ndembu of Zambia*. Cornell, NY: Cornell University Press.

6
ARCHETYPAL GRIEF OF AFRICAN AMERICAN WOMEN

Family

Four sons and one daughter
are born to my mother
we are birthed close,
colors of woven cloth
seamlessly mating
each has something of our mother,
the quickness of her walk brings my sister to market,
faster, better able to get the best grains, the best cloth,
the eldest brother smiles and convinces men
who would never part with their herd
to take less in exchange,
my second brothers, same twins as my two sons
provide our
village with twice the healing,
they open our path to Ogun
across our foreheads run the mark of our family,
we are known and loved by this sign,
it marks us as blood,
it marks us as family

Fanny Brewster
Journey: The Middle Passage

The mirror as whole

The archetypal grief of African American women at child loss begins in the African motherland. From this place, millions of Africans came to the Americas as slaves.

But before they were taken on those ships, what was life like for them, for the men and women in these villages? Before I add the Jungian language that will come later, I would like for us to imagine life back then—in an African setting. The importance of this imagining cannot be overstated because one of the most important reasons slavery succeeded was by creating a European story that intentionally chose not to see Africanist people as culturally vibrant and alive, on a path that was inherently good and natural for them. Before the slave ships came and took mothers and fathers away from their children, sold these children into slavery, there were families. There is a reason, a cause, that contributes to archetypal grief and it is due fundamentally to the creation of a false historical narrative of a de-valued African motherland, where there exists no psyche, no imaginal, except in service of the European-created "primitive."

There has been a historical deprecation of African countries as well as the enslaved Africanist birth mothers who were separated from their children. The importance of remembering an imaginal African psyche in all its beauty and with all of its potentiality is necessary. It is important to remember that African Americans had and can claim that place of the African motherland—as a location in the Africanist psyche as seen by Africanist cultural consciousness.

The ease with which African American families could be broken up and sold over hundreds of years happened partially because the concept of them as family had to be eliminated. This was accomplished immediately by separating these family members one from another. It was done before departure on the slave ships, at the auction blocks in America, and on the plantations. Families were sometimes allowed to remain together, but it was for the financial benefit of the slaveholder.

Within the African family and the community, rituals were respected. One of the significant aspects of Jungian psychology that made it so acceptable to many was its view and acceptance of mythology. We are fascinated by stories of our heroes and heroines. Each story gives us the specific rituals that we remember and come to expect in the story telling. Each African village had its story teller—its *griot*. Each African village had its rituals and customs.

I would like to share with you part of a writing I completed in honor of those who died in the Katrina storm of Louisiana. It is called *Katrina: Water and Sacred Rites*. In this writing, I speak about an aspect of early life in Africa—the baptism blessing. This is about the Senegalese. The children are named one week after their birth. Parents and family gather to participate in the rites and rituals of the child, carried out by sacred water. It is most often mixed with plant leaves or roots to create a tonic specific to the protection and wisdom of the mother and child as with the rat plant.

Every aspect of the new life of the child is marked with rites that have been passed on for generations.

These birth and naming rites are sacred as each name has meaning based on many possibilities: the day of the week, the noted child's personality, or a grandparent whom the child resembles in affect.

On the appointed day, the child's mother extinguishes the fire and sweeps the house and *takes a bath* and the baby is *washed with the medicinal water*. These are symbolic acts marking the end of one phase of life and the beginning of a new one…. In the center of the compound, a mat is spread where an old woman, usually the midwife, sits with the child on her lap. The child is shaved, starting on the right side. Nearby stands a clay bowl with red and white kola nuts, cotton, and millet. The red kola nuts symbolize long life, and the white ones symbolize good luck. *An elderly person rubs their hands over the child's head, prays and spits in its ears to implant the name in the baby's head.* After that, the name is then announced loudly to the crowd, and prayers are offered for long life and prosperity. The child and mother are hidden away if it is the first born, in case someone with an evil eye should see them.

Life in Africa had its own life rhythms and patterns. Kohut and others have spoken about the necessity for mirroring in the life of the child. Each member of African societies was actually engaged in mirroring long before the term acquired usage in American psychological circles. African cultures thrived for centuries living from one generation to another using what we have later given psychological language to—such as mirroring. This historical African mirroring is shown then as we see it now in the present day by the lives of those who lived in those times. One such person was Olaudah Equiano, a former slave who wrote an autobiography, *The Interesting Narrative of the Life of Olaudah Equiano*, in 1789. His is one of the first stories of former slaves to give us the rich details of precolonial life in Africa:

> As I was the youngest of the sons, I became, of course, the greatest favourite with my mother, and was always with her; and she tried to take particular pains to form my mind. I was trained up from my earliest years in the art of war; my daily exercise shooting and throwing javelins; and my mother adorned me with emblem, after the manner of our greatest warriors. In this way I grew up till I was turned the age of eleven, when an end was put to my happiness.
>
> *(Equiano, 1789, p. 32)*

Mirroring

The effects of mirroring determine our self-concept, how we can be with others in empathy and how we learn to thrive through the mutual experience of understanding others. The life that African children had with their parents allowed them to live a whole, full life. We do not have in-depth psychological studies of precolonial life, but we do have knowledge of how villages functioned socially, spiritually, and creatively. These give us valuable clues as to the strong possibility of how mirroring, without it being termed that, was relevant and present in the lives of Africans.

Olaudah's story is not one of the pain or suffering of being an African village child. It is one that describes his normal life, living in a particular culture at a particular time, until this life was disrupted by his being kidnapped and put into slavery.

I imagine that prior to arriving at the coast, Olaudah's early life in Africa was one of play, love, and a family and mothering experience with which we ourselves are familiar. It has been centuries since he wrote his autobiography, but what makes him real to me, and perhaps to you, is the humanity of his story—of this early life. Most of us know what it is to play, to laugh, and to be present with someone. Olaudah, like us, had this someone whom he called mother, who reflected him in all things.

Our mothers are the earliest bright mirror that reflects back to us who we will become in life. The relationship we have with this woman sets us on a life path that is sometimes rocky, sometimes painful and, we hope, beautiful. We need our mothers. If we cannot have them because of their early deaths or illness, we *still* feel the loss of our birth mothers.

Much of what we experience in the clinical setting and the work that we do there is about the relationship we have had or not had with our mothers. A great deal of it is about longing for what we did not get and the painful acceptance of what will never be as time has passed. We come to learn as we deepen this psychological work that it is also not just the relationship with our birth mothers that has great significance but also the relationship that she has had with her own mother. It is an intergenerational experience of mothering that has created the people we are, sitting together in a quiet room, trying to untangle the web of emotional pain in which we find ourselves. We come to learn, as both analysts and patients, that the analysis we come to trust is helping us to see, feel, and become mother in whatever unique healing ways we require.

Defining the archetypal

We begin with defining the archetype and the archetypal. As Jungians, we want to take our lead from Jung. This makes sense, so let's begin with a few of his words from the section "Psychological Aspects of the Mother Archetype" in *Aspects of the Feminine*. Then we will move to slavery as an archetypal event, then to the individuals who live with this particular archetypal energy in the experience of archetypal grief.

> Like any other archetype, the mother archetype appears under an almost infinite variety of aspects. I mention here only some of the more characteristic. First in importance are the personal mother and grandmother, stepmother and mother-in-law; then any woman with whom a relationship exists—for example a nurse or governess or perhaps a remote ancestress. Then there are what might be termed mothers in a figurative sense. To this category belongs the goddess, and especially the Mother of God, the Virgin, and Sophia. Mythology offers many variations of the mother archetype.
>
> (CW 9i, Para. 156)

Slavery as an archetypal event

Jung says, "The existence of the instincts can no more be proved than the existence of the archetypes, so long as they do not manifest themselves concretely."

We know from this statement that the form in which slavery fits has a historical presence.

People have enslaved each other for a very long time in one way or another. I believe that slavery is an archetypal event because the form of slavery does exist in our psyches. We can see this in modern times as more children and women and sometimes men are taken into modern-day slavery. The words *human bondage* now more often make us think of individuals taken as sex slaves. If slavery is an archetypal event, what of those who participate in such an event—the slaves as well as those who enslave them? What of their emotional experiences at being slaves? Do these also not take on an archetypal affect fitting into the form of archetype?

Defining archetypal grief: mother of sorrows

My patient sits with me crying in a way that seems beyond any human suffering. I cannot comfort her. She is beyond my reach of nurturance-giving. I deeply feel her pain and anguish. I have known her sorrow. I understand that she isn't crying because of the death of her biological mother, who does still live.

Hers is the archetypal, intergenerational mourning for the passing of all failed mother-nurturance. This inevitable failure has occurred not because of anything my patient has done wrong, nor her mother before her. It is rather a result of the horrible success of slavery.

The sadness shown by my patient is indicative of the depth of our grief as African American women, as we try to find a connection, a reflection of ourselves in the archetypal mirror of mothering.

One of the long-term effects of American slavery is that it severely damaged the natural line of maternal instinct of the relationship between African American mothers and their children. The event of slavery, I believe, transformed our consciousness in how we conceive, birth, and raise our children. Equally important, it put African American women on a journey of archetypal grief that remains with us today.

We all need nurturance, and the first bond of this nurturance comes at the breast, from our mothers. What happens when we do not—cannot—get this nurturance because mothering is unavailable? Sometimes we can get it through the maternal line due to grandmotherly love and attention, but what if even this is absent?

I'm considering the absence of the mothering we require due to societal and cultural conditions that date back to American slavery.

As I sit and live with and through the emotional trauma of women crying their sorrow, I am reminded of how African American women have a tragic absence of the mother due to slavery. I believe that those days of punishing terror, when African American children were taken away from their mothers and sold into slavery, continue to haunt us.

There is a thread of tapestry, of grief, that is almost inconsolable which runs through our longing to be loved and nurtured. When the lines of mother nurturing are so tragically broken by a 400-year event such as American slavery, it could be expected that the healing from such an event could take double that number of years.

We are not there yet, and I witness this in African and Caribbean women crying with all the sadness of mother loss, as if they themselves have just been sold off to a distant plantation.

In reflecting on African American women like Diane who see me weekly for analytical work, I consider their mother complexes not only within the context of ego potentialities and neuroses but also within the cultural context of the African American life. This life has included a post-traumatic experience of slavery that can be remembered on a cellular level. The trauma of slavery and its aftermath lives in the conscious awareness of African Americans on a daily basis.

This is not only because we can read about it in history books or hear stories about slavery. It is because a key component of the African American experience of racism continues until today. If we consider how this trauma has affected African Americans in a broad way, what might become even more apparent on a microscopic level is the trauma of the separation of mother and child due to the conditions of slavery. How do we heal ourselves of the images of children being birthed, *bred*, and sold as human cattle for the survival of the plantation system?

It is almost still intolerable to imagine, and the Emancipation Proclamation took place over 100 years ago. Yet there is still the interweaving of these birthed slave children, their fate, and my African American women clients that continues to cause the suffering of mother loss as experienced today.

African American women live with the spirits of history. All of the children that were lost to slavery—taken away, murdered, beaten—are still within the cultural consciousness of African Americans. The women who are working on their deep sadness, for which they cannot find a source, are in remembrance of their own mother loss as well as all the women who lost their children to slavery for over 400 years. When I hear them cry in our sessions together, I can sense the presence of these children—as I can feel the grief of the woman who sits with me, trying to understand how her life is apparently going so well and how she can still be so sad as if her mother had just died.

One of the major issues of working with African American women like Diane is finding a place to rest within the analytical work that allows for grief, not only at the recognition of the breakage of the maternal mirror of present time but also of the mourning that must take place for the loss of all the children in the past. This loss of the child includes my client, who oftentimes has no recognition of her own inner child.

The language itself and talk of an inner child can cause discomfort. A large and oftentimes difficult aspect of accepting life as an African American woman is having to grow up too fast. The inner child barely has time to be a child.

This is not unlike the young slave child, especially the female child, who could be raped or "trained" at an early age to make themselves the *pillow* or *bed warmer* for White men or women. In the buried side of consciousness, where we hide all the collective and individual remembrances of slavery in order to survive, is the painful forgetfulness of being an African American child. These residual, mostly forgotten, memories of slavery still live within on a cultural level.

When African American women cry about the absence of their mothers in their current lives, when they see how limited is the affection and contact they can have with their living mothers, when they feel abandoned by mothers who they still see every week or with whom they sit and have meals—these are the ghosts of children lost and mothers' sorrow at slavery, which trapped them in African American consciousness centuries ago.

The feeling of abandonment that patients have appears archetypal. Their mothers are still alive, they still see them, and yet the sense of loss is profound. The shift in the phenomenological field is profound as we live together, struggling for life together, as if once again experiencing the death of the mother. I say it is archetypal because it comes from that place that doesn't only know the number of slaves brought over during the Middle Passage or the number of slaves birthed and sold into slavery, but rather that power of *knowing* of the deepest sense of loss of the children.

Post-traumatic slave syndrome is defined by author Joy DeGruy as multigenerational trauma together with continued oppression, and an absence of opportunity to access the benefits available in the society.

She says that the resulting behaviors are (1) *vacant esteem*—which has to do with health; (2) *ever-present anger*; and (3) *racist socialization*. I connect these behaviors when thinking of Diane and her suffering.

Patient case narrative: introduction

Now I would like to share with you about Diane, one of the patients I have worked with in the past few years. As I tell you about her, I want you to consider mirroring, and I also want you to consider what we have come to label *attachment disorders*. I want you to also think about racial complexes. The attachment disorder deals with the relationship between a child and her caregiver. This initial relationship, usually with the mother, will have certain characteristics that are identifiable in later life and can be seen in adult life. Two main possibilities exist in terms of how the *Diagnostic and Statistical Manual of Mental Disorders* (DSM) broadly defines attachment disorders. In the first, reactive attachment disorder (RAD), the child has not been able to have a consistent relationship with the main caregiver. Due to this inconsistency, the child grows up not trusting and having confidence that there will be someone there for her. The early attachment is insecure and, as a result, the adult who has this early experience can spend a great deal of life avoiding the painful experience of the anxiety and fear of not having anyone, as we would say, "show up for them."

The other form of attachment disorder is called *disinhibited social engagement disorder* or DSED. In this case, children have had multiple caregivers, and a major characteristic of the disorder is that early life has been constantly disrupted with a number of different caregivers.

The child has not had the ability to create a pattern of expectation that one person will be there to provide consistent comforting, nurturing, and soothing. As grown-up adults, these children will seek their comfort wherever they can get it. Relationships are not trusting or binding, and temporality is a key feature.

Now, I would like to add something about African American mothers and daughters in light of mirroring and attachment. My first thoughts are actually questions. How might slavery affect a mother's relationship with her children? How does attachment disorder and lack of mirroring result in the inconsolable despair being seen in African American women? We know that American slavery was cruel in its willingness to sell children away from their mothers. The possibilities of centuries-long separation over generations would create a hole, an emptiness that might be impossible to fill. This is a part of archetypal grieving. The despair is so deep and extended over time that all ego consciousness regarding the reason for such a sense of emptiness, in the face of having a present birth mother, could only be archetypal. Does such an experience of such great separation create its own archetypal circumstance or birth? Where have we seen such a happening? Does this situation bring into existence a new archetypal energy created by particular energies brought together by the disruption of mothering in the lineage of African American women and their children?

The following words are from the story of a former slave girl growing up in Bermuda during the early nineteenth century. The book is *Six Women's Slave Narratives*. The author of this story is a young girl by the name of Mary Prince, who was born around 1810 to a household slave mother and a slave ship carpenter. Her story begins with a brief history of her life. I will share with you from when she discovers she is to be sold away at age 11 from her parents and the White family she has lived with almost since birth.

> The black morning at length came; it came too soon for my poor mother and us. Whilst she was putting on us the new *osnaburgs* in which we were to be sold, she said, in a sorrowful voice (I shall never forget it!) "See, I am shrouding my poor children: what a task for a mother.... At length the vendue master, who was to offer us for sale like sheep or cattle, arrived, and asked my mother which was the eldest. She said nothing, but pointed to me. He took me by the hand, and led me out into the middle of the street.... I was soon surrounded by strange men, who examined and handled me in the same manner that a butcher would a calf or a lamb he was about to purchase, and who talked about my shape and size in like words—as if I could not more understand their meaning than the dumb beasts. The bidding commenced and gradually rose to fifty-seven (38lbs. sterling).... I then saw my sisters led forth and sold to different owners.... It was a sad parting; one went one way, one another, and our poor mammy went home with nothing.
>
> (Prince, 1988, pp. 2–3)

Patient case narrative: self-description

Diane is now 39 years of age. At the time of our first session, she had just turned 33. Diane is ethnically a mixture of African American and Native American. She is extremely slightly built in terms of bone structure but appears taller—approximately 5'9", for what may be her weight. Diane has a ruddy, light skin complexion and shoulder-length, curly brown hair. Diane walks with slightly sloped shoulders, almost with a hump in her back. Her body language suggests defeat and intensity as shown by her almost stomp-like walk. She has long fingers that are generally at rest and which she rarely uses to express herself. Her body is still, almost rigid in its lack of movement.

From our initial contact until we terminated therapy, Diane worked at a local sports arena as a private room seasonal hostess. In addition, she is an unpaid intern with a local actors' group. Diane has a BFA degree in Theatre Arts/Acting, which she received in 1998.

Diane has held the intern position for four years, and she considers it to be a "big opportunity" for her to become a professional member of the group and learn her art as an actor. She and I both consider her to be underemployed in her profession.

Diane described herself as someone who had a great deal of difficulty "sharing" who she was with others. She stated that she did not like to talk about herself and preferred to focus on the other person rather than herself. She also described herself as being very passive even though her professional life required her to be a great deal more active. She felt herself to be "uncomfortable" in her own skin and has always had "low self-esteem."

Diane stated that she wanted to be a "successful, working actor" and she wanted to "get out of her own way." Though she stated she would rather "focus on others," she is estranged from her biological family with the exception of her mother, with whom she has a minimal telephone conversation once a month. Diane has only one friend named John, who referred her to the referral service.

The initial dream is used as an important aspect of comparative analysis in Jungian work in ascertaining the nature of the presenting problem. When evaluated, this dream is capable of giving not only diagnosis within a Jungian context for the psychological work but also has prognostic markers for the nature and possible outcome of this work. It also may provide a view of the nature of the transference in the patient–therapist process.

Diane has experienced the introjections of her mother and father—repressed rage, depression, isolation, passivity, and an unfocused sense of life purpose. All of these features cause in Diane an undeveloped persona, poor ego strength for meeting basic material needs, and an inability to go deeper inside herself and imagine on a symbolic level. Diane offered her presenting problems as an inability to relate to others, self-imposed isolation, and "melancholy." She also stated she had low self-esteem.

The lack of mirroring caused ego impoverishment. She stated she was passive but needed to be more active in terms of pursuing her life as an actress. In our work together, Diane can be very hostile, with angry outbursts against me. She calls me "stupid" and "ignorant" when she is feeling particularly angry about one of my interpretations or comments. I believe that this display is indicative of the repressed anger and rage that Diane holds resulting from her negative father complex. Her alcoholic father would visit Diane's family only a few times a month. Other times he worked in the city away from Diane, her mother, and her seven siblings.

Diane observed her father hitting and verbally abusing her mother throughout her childhood until she was 16, when her father permanently moved in with his city "family"—another wife and four other children. Diane would hide when her father came home and began his abuse. She oftentimes would avoid the other children and her mother even when her father was gone from the home. Her mother, as an abused woman and mother of eight, was rarely available to be with Diane. The "melancholy" that Diane presents with is reminiscent of the depression of the battered female.

The low self-esteem experienced by Diane's mother is clearly seen in Diane through her cluttering and the "mess" she lives in, and the verbal and sometimes physical abuse she receives from her friend John is another indicator of this low self-esteem.

Diane's sometimes poor, disrespectful treatment at the actors' studio is another example of a place where Diane is scapegoated as an intern but where she fails to see the relationship between her background and her presenting. In session when she screams at me that she is "not a door mat," I can see the ego's regressive defense and the anger substituting for sadness. My clinical experiences note the following:

1. Diane does not consider herself to be a "victim." She insists that I am pushing this onto her because I believe she is a "door mat."
2. She is only now beginning to see how what she calls her "damage" as a child actually belongs to her.
3. Diane's experience of her father's abuse and her mother's victimization has been very painful to confront, never mind accept.
4. She has been unable to tolerate due to emotional pain and unable to access dissociated experiences or share much of her background information with me. We have spent a little more than two years with her insisting that she doesn't "like to talk about herself."

In the many moments of silence we have spent with each other in session, I am left to imagine and surmise her sense of painful silence and isolation in her childhood home.

1. Her silence with me is not only representative of this but also of the angry rejection (projecting negative mother onto me) she gives me in these regressive periods.
2. Diane has shown very poor adaptation to her life as an adult. She exhibits most of her childhood trauma issues as an adult.
3. John is her only friend. She has no social life and spends only time outside of her apartment to work.

Diane began her therapeutic work with presenting problems involving a Jungian diagnostic understanding of ego/self-axis, shadow, persona, ego structure, negative parental complexes, archetypal defenses, Narcissus, inferiority complex, and rigid ego structure. Other elements were low self-esteem, depression, isolation, and a passive stance in life.

She lacked good enough ego strength to take care of herself and had poor persona development. All of these issues show themselves in a diagnostic understanding of a borderline personality with narcissistic tendencies which she exhibits in our therapeutic relationship and her encounters with others. Her own self-hatred and rigid defense system disallows her from bonding with others and forces her to make them bad objects. Her very weak social skills reflect an undeveloped persona. Her reliance on silence and adamant refusal to initiate conversation throughout our session points to an understanding of her preverbal emotional state and the desire to be totally taken care of in a way that likely did not occur in her child rearing due to the stress placed on her overly burdened mother.

Within a model that acknowledges archetypal grief, several factors have influenced Diane in the development of her personality: a disconnection between ego and the unconscious, which affects her spirituality; a lack of effective mothering, especially mirroring; and the intergenerational racial trauma of her mother line. Diane exists: A smart young woman from an ethnic lineage who seems unable to move through the trauma of her self-perception of collective racism that exists against her as a woman of color actor.

The fragmented mirror: slavery

Patient case narrative: a Jungian clinical picture

Psychoanalytically, from a Jungian perspective, Diane's presenting problems show a disconnection between her ego and her unconscious. The isolation that she feels internally, and which is reinforced by her lack of relationship with others, is an indication and a mirror of her inability to access herself in a symbolic manner.

She has mostly been intolerant of any touching on the areas of unconscious materials—fantasy, dreams, active imagination, or imaginal play. Diane has a rigid ego structure that tends to move into the defenses of regression or projective identification. She has a very poorly developed persona. She is very limited in social skills—conversational or dialogue—and lacks an emotional range of expressed feelings. Diane tends to rely on anger as a defense in avoiding dealing with feelings of sadness or other painful emotional states. This anger gets directed at others in her environment, whom, until quite recently, she referred to as pigeons. She described herself as the "rare bird."

In Jungian terms, a presenting problem represents a symptom, a metaphor, a symbol for a dis-ease between the ego and the self—the unconscious that would be a source for growth and transformation. Her lack of ability to engage with herself on the deeper unconscious level, having a poor persona and being unwilling to explore negative father and mother complexes, creates a problem for growth on a path of individuation.

Because Diane cannot connect her ego difficulties with a teleological perspective of the archetypal, she is angry, frustrated, and afraid. Her early childhood trauma of alcoholic father and battered mother has created an intrapsychic state that mirrors the early childhood trauma and places her in a constant state of combat with a strong archetypal defense. She is often torn, feeling the internal split between the "good" that she wants to achieve in her life and the "bad" that she encounters whenever she (her ego) moves in the direction of realizing her professional objectives.

Diane shows up for treatment because she cannot understand her life in a way that gives meaning and purpose. The presenting problem, if understood from a depth psychological perspective, defines and gives clarity to what the patient cannot trace due to any possible reason but is specific to that patient. These reasons may include, as with Diane, a disconnection between ego and unconscious. It may be a "flooding" by the unconscious where the patient experiences dissociation as a way of life or depression where there is no relief from Hades and life in the underworld.

The movement of the Jungian psychological work is downward to the psyche, returning with information which is significant for the ego to understand, integrate, and make use of.

In this way, the presenting problem reflects not just the singular aspects of ego (the need for food, shelter, work, etc.) but also gives direction as to the self-related problem of the individual who, Jung believed, could only attain some life satisfaction from being on a path of individuation. *Individuation* means a teleological understanding of why one has life, the inner-directed use of unconscious material from the self in support of continued ego development in support of this life.

Viewed from an African American psychological perspective, with consideration of the effects of post-traumatic slave syndrome on Diane, how do we interpret who she appears to be? Can we add another dimension of understanding to who she is and how she functions in the world based on her present life and the ethnic lineage from which she descends? She has no plans to have children. None of the African American women with whom I work plan on having children of their own. They have all stated in one way or another that they feel the burden of their own lives is too great to become mothers of African American children.

Mother of Sorrows is one of the many names for the Virgin Mary in the Catholic tradition. Her deep sorrow is the loss of her son, Jesus. Erzulie Ferda is from an Africanist tradition—also a mother of sorrows. If we think about the archetypal mother, then we can see the energy of the archetypal grief shown to us through the image of the Mother of Sorrows. Once again, I reference Karla Holloway in *Moorings and Metaphors*, which addressed African American women's literature, focusing on mythology from an Africanist perspective. In her introduction, the author defined moorings as "where behavior, art, philosophy and language unite as a cultural expression within an African-American literary tradition" (Holloway, 1992, p. 1).

Holloway's primary thrust was to identify the common ways of knowing and the resultant framing of language that exist in the writings of Africanist women. The author described "metaphor" as soul and as gender and goddess or ancestor. She saw a bridge between African spirituality and African American writers' call to the goddess in their writings.

Three contextual perspectives of mythology include revision, remembrance, and recursion. The author discussed each perspective, noting the difference between "recovery" and "retrieval." Black women have been able to recover the soul or self that has been lost through colonization by writing and taking the "word" as their own. However, she said, "All that was buried in colonial Africa—language, religion, political independence, economic policy—was lost by enslaved Africans.

Retrieval for Africans means an overthrow of power and a reinvestment in self-determination. For the African-American, retrieval is not possible. Instead, recovery means an act of spiritual memory rather than physical possession" (Holloway, 1992, p. 20). In continuing, Holloway observed that Black women writers have the goddess or mother spirit at the center of most of their writings.

The spiritual memory of which Holloway speaks reminds me of the archetypal possibilities that we all have through the spiritual memory of the unconscious.

Remembering through stories and myths becomes a method of psychological renewal where a reframing of life and identity occurs in a spontaneous way, at the will of psyche. Holloway, by using Black women writers, provided another avenue for looking at mythology, recognizing the legacy of the African oral tradition while accepting the phenomenological experiences of contemporary life. A blending of the mythic old with the new is essential not only for creating a dialectic but for moving the mythic story forward and giving it new life rituals. The act of writing and reframing of traditional stories allows for participation in an ancient African ritual.

Holloway began her initial exploration of myth by investigating and developing her concept of remembrance. She believed that "memory is culturally inscribed.... This kind of inscription is assigned to the genre of myth" (1992, p. 24).

Holloway said of myth that it is a dynamic entity that "(re)members community, connects it to the voices from which it has been severed and forces it out of the silence prescribed by a scriptocentric historicism" (1992, p. 25). According to Holloway, myth is a cultural memory, belonging to both the spiritual and physical worlds and is "a collective linked by story and traditions."

The sons

What has become of the male children of these archetypally grief-stricken women? Not just back then in the days following the Reconstruction when African American men were coerced and entrapped into providing work service by false arrest charges and forced prison sentences that provided unpaid labor for companies.

What has become of the modern-day African American man? Fifty-four percent of them make up the prison population system. We seem to live with the unconscious expectation that African American men can be dismissed. Dismissed from being cared about, dismissed by being made to be men to be afraid of, dismissed from having a life of value. Numerous authors and African American men have written and spoken about the fear they see in others at their approach.

I recognize this fear of me in others at times when I am mistaken for male because of my short hair and my height. White women actually holding their purses closer, policemen who have stopped me for a real or imagined traffic violation unable to hide their surprise that I am an African American female and not male.

We have psychologically thrown them away long before they become members of the prison class. It begins early in elementary school. I believe in the large urban schools that educate our children, there can be such a lack of care, a refusal to be optimistic for these children on the part of some teachers, that continuously supports the creation, the preparation of the prison class. These teachers are afraid to care. They want their pensions, their lives with their own families, their security.

They cannot afford to have seen within themselves or the children sitting in front of them the understated suffering in which we all live. Perhaps, if they could see, they would not be able to rise each morning and enter their classrooms. But is it their job alone to protect these children? Isn't their job only to teach? Isn't it why they went to school—to become teachers? Most of them make the decision to do this—to stay committed to their role, their livelihood, to live out what they have trained for—to be good teachers, all the while in the face of failing students.

It is not their fault. The teachers have walked into a part of the social system that prepares many students for failure, not success. The teachers want to be awake but can only be this awake for their own families. The Shadow of not seeing and forgetfulness remains too strong for them to increase the light shine of awareness.

Jung says that our job is to move out of the darkness, to shine the light on those places where we are in the dark. How many centuries must we endure being in such a nigredo place of consciousness as regards the constant re-creation of an African American class of men whose only destiny is prison?

I want to address the issue of these grown-up African American boys who become men. It is obvious, the effects on them of the archetypal patterns of American slavery, which appear to renew themselves in each new generation. It would be impossible for mothers to carry the burden of grief as I have described without their sons being affected. It appears that the most significant recognition of the effects of this grief is for society to build more prisons.

The Black Lives Matter movement has been successful up to this point because it makes visible the killing of African American men by police violence in a highly visible way. Over a period of several months during this last year, each month, African American men or boys were being killed by policemen. This is a fact of American life—this is not a myth, though it sometimes appears mythological.

The mirror's poor repair: Reconstruction and beyond

The psychology of survival for African American women and their children

What does it mean to survive? When I speak with my patients about how they had to make adjustments to life with their parents, how they had to sacrifice parts of themselves in order to live, they nod in recognition. They breathe deeply in acknowledging that my words are finally allowing them to be seen. I can mirror to them their own personal anxiety at having to hide themselves for decades.

When you are caught in a complex, you are hidden from yourself. I imagine the ways in which African Americans had to hide in order to survive. Hiding was a key component of being able to continue living. Over the hundreds of years that slavery existed and the years after—the Reconstruction years—how did hiding support survival? What impact did this have on the African American psyche?

Ralph Ellison wrote a landmark book about African Americans titled *Invisible Man*. The wish for others to make African Americans invisible in a way almost matches the latter's wish to be invisible for the sake of survival. But I think there is something in human nature that cannot allow this. We are forced out of our places of hiding because we need to be seen and to be heard. It begins at a young age and continues, hopefully, for a lifetime. This need to give voice to our rage, sadness, and disappointments is what brings patients into our offices; oftentimes, it is what has brought us to our calling as analysts.

Patient case narrative: survival

We must survive. Diane came to do analytical work with me because something in her wanted to survive. When she would speak about why she came to do our work together, she said it was because of John, her friend. He sent her, made her come. Over time, she would listen to me say that she actually kept coming on her own so that he was not given all the credit for her work.

When Diane began making attempts to leave our work, I had a secret wish for her to remain longer. She had begun to understand some things about herself and was not so enraged that her color was a factor in getting the acting roles she wanted. Her affect was sometimes lively; she smiled more frequently. She had stopped saying she wanted to take a bat and beat me over my head. Some things had changed. I didn't think it was enough, and I wanted her to stay longer.

Diane was still only speaking to her mother once a month—the obligatory Sunday afternoon phone call. She had made no contact with any of her siblings during the years we worked together. However, she was attempting to take an acting class and a swimming class—to participate in group activities.

Diane showed classic post-traumatic slave syndrome. Her concept of herself lacked esteem and showed ever-present anger and racist socialization. In our work together, I could think about and feel into those places that showed the features of this syndrome. Some might argue for the dominance of a Jungian diagnostic interpretation alone or one of borderline from the DSM. But in my experiences of sitting in the room, being in the field, I know that there is a presence of the past, the spirit of what is the trauma of slavery and its lingering grief and as seen in Diane—its rage.

The personal archetypal mother

In *Oya: In Praise of the Goddess*, discussing the personal Orisha and relationship with archetypal energy author Judith Gleason says:

> What is at issue here is the extent to which the worshiper of an Orisha has been able to integrate the archetypal force into her total personality structure. When one is not aware of the presence of the Orisha in everyday life, then

> chances are the split in the inner world has not been healed. The Orisha possessing the person remains autonomous.... The Orisha mirrors the hidden self.... In the European process of psychoanalysis it is up to the client to find words to tell who she really is.... In the African system it is the oracle with the diviner as intermediary who tells the person who she really is. The Self speaks through the cowries, interpreted by the spiritual counselor.
>
> *(Gleason, 1987, p. 261)*

I do believe that we need archetypal mothers of our own to help us really live, find out who we really are, and go beyond survival in this life. In my work with African American women, there is an immense need for what we call *ego strengthening*.

I find that the ego is already in such a deflated place that almost the immediate focus is on helping the patient see a little light out of the darkness. To feel into herself as not being vacant, empty. Just as important is a sense of the Orisha, an archetypal mother energy.

I would like to share with you a section of a reading from a manuscript I have written. It is about what I had first called the *shadow of creativity*. It's about procrastination and is actually a workbook for making changes in oneself in this area.

The imaginal is very important. I have used Jung's active imagination to further my self-understanding and to heal places that were deeply wounded from childhood. The adoption of an archetypal mother has had an immense impact on my psyche and strengthening my own ego. So I will share with you some of my personal process in this work.

> Kali is a Divine Mother goddess in India whose name means for truth. One of the derivatives of her name is Time. The day I indicated to my analyst that Kali was the image which had come to me, we discussed some of the power of Kali.
>
> My unconscious produced this goddess. I had no images or books about Kali before saying her name that day. Since then I have explored her mythology. I have found that she is the Mother who fiercely protects and guards. She is usually pictured with a necklace of skulls.
>
> Her skirt can be made out of human arms. Snakes are her bracelets. Wow! I didn't plan on this kind of support but there it was, the exact kind of archetypal mother I required to help me build and protect my emotional foundation as an adult.
>
> Creation and destruction are the qualities represented by Kali's four arms. These are qualities which ebb and flow in my work as writer–artist. I must constantly have an eye to creation—beginning my work and the destruction–revision. Some writers believe that revising the work is the true art form.
>
> All artists must learn to tolerate throwing away or changing that which does not fit, doesn't move the work forward.
>
> When I procrastinate I am also creating and destroying. But I am creating and re-creating habits which lower my self-esteem and how and what I think about myself, this is self-destructive. It is difficult to feel good about me

when I don't keep my own appointment time for sitting down to write. I don't think so well of myself when I stand my dentist up. He took care of me when I called at 1:00 a.m. with a dental emergency. Now that's over, I don't feel so pressured to keep my regular cleaning appointment—which would have helped me avoid that emergency appointment if I had kept my regular one! It starts getting a bit twisted. But if I can begin honoring the truth that Kali stands for, I will arrive at promised destinations and on time.

Another of the features of Kali is her association with mortality. She is an avid reminder to me of the limitation of life. It is very brief. Sometimes, I look up at the stars and realize that the starlight I see was sent hundreds or thousands of years ago. The star itself may already have disappeared from the galaxy. My life is important and my life is also short. Hanging out in the shadows of avoidance of life through delay and postponement, only shortens my life even more.

It is ironic, because it looks as if I have more time because I have postponed some inevitable task or responsibility. The truth is that the task will probably still have to be completed. Another truth, is that it will actually take me longer, with a greater loss of life energy because I delayed. After my imaging Kali, I understood better the importance of living each moment more fully. This is an impossibility when I am procrastinating. It is impossible to live fully, while hiding behind avoidance. Life requires full engagement. Otherwise it is not life, it is self destruction.

Therapist-authors Leslie Jackson and Beverly Greene have written about the psychological work that needs to happen with African American women in order to promote successful healing. I agree with the authors' conceptual framework in their book *Psychotherapy with African American Women: Innovations in Psychodynamic Perspectives and Practice*, and I always attempt to bring to the Jungian lens the lived experiences of an African American woman.

The Bridge

It's the water that first catches your eyes.
You barely glance at the simple bridge arching itself across the North Canadian River.
Sunlight shimmers on water, holding an intense glow that says it must be late morning.
Trees on both sides of the banks are in full bloom.
White men, women and children stand on the bridge, some bending over the railing, to watch what swings below, as river water flows soft as tears.
If you look closer, you can see what photographer G. H. Farnum caught, reflected,
on the river's water. The two photographic down river views of this scene are historical, and known as Farnum's number 2899 and number 2897.
He was late.

Hundreds had already seen the image he made famous that day.

What hangs off the bridge deck, catching the photographer's eyes on May 25, 1911, was not such an uncommon sight and yet the standing bridge viewers probably thought themselves lucky, to be captured in the frame of the camera's eye.

In that moment, the photographer caught the trees, the shiny river, the blossoming river bank shrubs, and all 35 men, 6 women and 17 children who came to see the lynched Laura Nelson, and her fourteen year old son LD.

That bridge, from that day, in that place, Okemah, Oklahoma, is no longer there.

It has been replaced by another, but this is the one we see:
Raped mother hangs across from her son.
They face one another, rope tight around their necks,
caught forever in the shadow of the bridge.
Mother and son move with the breeze.
The sun shines.
Their shadows ripple
across flowing river water.
That bridge, from that day, in that place is no longer there,
yet this is the only one I can see.

Fanny Brewster
Journey: The Middle Passage

References

DeGruy, Joy. (2005). *Post Traumatic Slave Syndrome: America's Legacy of Enduring Injury and Healing*. Portland, OR: Joy DeGruy Publications.

Ellison, R. (1989). *Invisible Man*. New York: Vintage Books.

Equiano, Olaudah. (2001). *The Interesting Narrative of the Life of Olaudah Equiano*. Werner Sollors (ed.). New York: W.W. Norton & Company.

Gleason, Judith. (1987). *Oya: In Praise of the Goddess*. Boston, MA: Shambhala Publications.

Greene, Beverly and Leslie C. Jackson. (2000). *Psychotherapy with African American Women: Innovations in Psychodynamic Perspectives and Practice*. New York: Guilford Press.

Holloway, K. (1992). *Moorings and Metaphors: Figures of Culture and Gender in Black Women's Literature*. New Brunswick, NJ: Rutgers University Press.

Jung, C. G. (1968). *The Archetypes and the Collective Unconscious*. (*The Collected Works of C. G. Jung*, Vol. 9i). Princeton, NJ: Princeton University Press.

Kohut, Heinz. (2011). *The Search for the Self: Selected Writings of Heinz Kohut 1950–78*. London: Karnac Books.

Prince, Mary. (1988). *Six Women's Slave Narratives*. (*The Schomburg Library of Nineteenth-Century Black Women Writers*). New York: Oxford University Press.

7
THE JUNGIAN SHADOW

Dreaming the shadow

Jung speaks of the Shadow as that part of our psyche that is repressed and which we will not initially accept in our conscious states:

> This figure does not appear merely because it still exists in the individual, but because it rests on a dynamism whose existence can only be explained in terms of his actual situation, for instance because the shadow is so disagreeable to his ego-consciousness that it has to be repressed into the unconscious.
>
> *(CW 9i, Para. 474)*

Through the dreams, one is able to observe the personal Shadow and define its movement as it pushes us toward growth of the self. It is Jung's belief that first we must enter through the doorway of the Shadow before we are able to pass through to higher levels of development (anima/animus), leading to individuation. There are various resistances attached to the Shadow. Jung labels projections as "the most obstinate resistance" because it is very difficult for one to own and claim one's own defects and flaws.

In writing here about the Shadow, different aspects of this archetype will be discussed. My personal dreams are included for exploration of the Shadow on the personal/cultural level. In addition, the Shadow and its presence in collective American society is included as it is related to racism.

As an Africanist woman studying Jung's work and theories, it appeared necessary to me to address his work not only on a personal level through dreams but also on a broader cultural level. Jung, in speaking of Shadow projections, states, "No matter how obvious it may be to the neutral observer that it is a matter of projections, there is little hope that the subject will perceive this himself. He must be convinced that he throws a very long shadow before he is willing to withdraw his emotionally-toned projections from their object" (CW 9ii, Para.16).

For the past 20 years, there has been increased awareness of Jung's own Shadow as it relates to racism—for example, Farhad Dalal's article "Jung: A Racist." A few others have followed but none from the American Jungian analytical community, with the exception of Polly Young-Eisendrath. The most obvious discussions have centered, for the most part, on racism related to questions regarding Jung's suggested anti-Semitism, and this has emerged primarily from the European Jungian analytical community, with the exception of Jerome Bernstein.

I have found no in-depth exploration of Jung's theories discussed specifically in light of their relationship to African Americans with the exception of the work of Young-Eisendrath. Jung's words below from *Memories, Dreams, Reflections* provide some insight into why it is so essential for American Jungians to address his Shadow and Shadow projections.

Jung states:

> When the great night comes, everything takes on a note of deep dejection, and every soul is seized by an inexpressible longing for light. *That is the pent-up feeling that can be detected in the eyes of primitives, and also in the eyes of animals.* There is a sadness in animals' eyes, and we never know whether that sadness is bound up with the soul of the animal or is a poignant message which speaks to us out of that still unconscious existence.
>
> *(Jung, 1965, p. 269)*

In *Memories, Dreams, Reflections*, Jung's apparent view of the African is that he functions at a lower level of consciousness like that of animals. The above quote may appear to be an attempt at empathy, sadness, for the *primitive*, but it is absolutely racially negative to the human being. Africans being compared to animals with that same level of consciousness, as Jung experiences it through a look in their eyes, is racism at its worst.

This is not a moment that opens the heart, which is perhaps what Jung wished to convey. It is a moment of profound amazement that he would write such words.

Jung further states in discussing the Shadow archetype:

> Closer examination of the dark characteristics—that is, the inferiorities constituting the shadow reveals that they have an emotional nature, a kind of autonomy, and accordingly an obsessive or, better, possessive quality. Emotion, incidentally, is not an activity of the individual but something that happens to him. Affects occur usually where adaptation is weakest, namely a certain degree of inferiority and the existence of lower level of personality. On this lower level with its uncontrolled or scarcely controlled emotions one behaves more or less like a *primitive, who is not only the passive victim of his affects but also singularly incapable of moral judgment."*
>
> *(CW 9ii, Para. 474, italics added)*

The importance of exploring Jung's Shadow theory can be seen from varying perspectives. His theories have become more popular and widespread within American society. It appears to me that there is a danger in assuming in their entirety any one person's teachings without looking at the "shadow" of their work. I think this is especially true because of the nature of Jung's theories and his thoughts regarding Africans and individuals of Africanist descent. It somehow seems insufficient to me to say only that Jung was a "product of his times."

We are each a product of our times. The weight of Jung's own Shadow, extending from his time, is very heavy upon those of us of African descent and the American Jungian analytical community. As an African American woman exploring Jung's work, I proceed with extreme caution, having already been designated as the primitive functioning from a lower level of consciousness. As one reads Jung's writings, questions arise concerning the availability of the Other for increasing one's own power, recognition, whatever it is that the ego requires. What if there had been no "primitives" to hold the Shadow—the inferior? Where would Jung have placed his own need to be better, to have more consciousness than the "primitive"?

A second important reason for exploring Jung's theory of the Shadow is to bring fully to consciousness the task of making applicable Jung's theory regarding the Shadow, in recognizing that I, along with many *millions* of African descent, am a designated object of his own Shadow projection. As a dreamer and someone who studies dreams, I want to know, to understand how his theory meets my own actual experience of the dream including an awareness of cultural consciousness without racial bias. Because of this, it becomes more revealing and valuable to expand the exploration of the Shadow beyond the personal. Jung through his own unconscious and serving as one modern voice of the collective, has broadened and deepened the idea of Shadow in our unconscious selves.

He himself says, "It is quite within the bounds of possibility for a man to recognize the relative evil of his nature, but it is a rare and shattering experience for him to gaze into the face of absolute evil" (p. 10).

The absolute evil of the Shadow, according to Jung, then exists as archetypal. As related to Africanist people, he furthered the development of a racist archetype, a collective Shadow, a circumstance that he apparently neither recognized nor accepted.

Jung suggests that the Shadow, through its inescapable presence in our lives, promotes our growth toward wholeness. I believe this to be possible—that we live always seeking some inner peace that mirrors our vision of "wholeness." However, the importance of the work to be done on an individual level is not just in seeing the Shadow but also in claiming whatever personal "inferiorities" exist. Beyond this, it becomes equally important to be aware of the collective unconscious and how it influences our daily lives.

I believe that it is possible to influence the collective—the archetypal. This appears to be one of only a few ways in which to create major change in a society. This process begins at the personal, individual level. Jung's personal experience of his unconscious and his subsequent writings shows us an avenue for the possibility of psychological growth. However, like any road, there are imperfections and flaws. In his work, he points to and names the Shadow, but he leaves unclaimed a large portion of his own personal Shadow.

In *The Scapegoat Complex: Toward a Mythology of Shadow and Guilt,* Jungian analyst Sylvia Perera delves deeply into a discussion of what she calls the *scapegoat complex* and how it functions within us as individuals and part of a collective:

> We apply the term to individuals and groups who are accused of causing misfortune. This serves to relieve others, the scapegoaters, of their own responsibilities, and to strengthen the scapegoaters' sense of power and righteousness. In this current usage a search for the scapegoat relieves us also of our relationship to the transpersonal dimension of life, for in the present age we have come to function with a perverted form of the archetype, one that ignores the gods, and we blame the scapegoat and the devil for life's evils.
>
> (Perera, 1986, p. 8)

Perera says, "In Jungian terms, scapegoating is a form of denying the shadow of both man and God." This is one of the major issues that we face in working with the Jungian theoretical concept of Shadow. The inability to initially engage the Shadow archetype as it shows itself with the Jungian community, and the way in which it has been cast upon those belonging to non-White groups, directly addresses Perera's statement.

Personal dream

> I am in a house with a center. The house is shaped like the letter H. On the upper right side of the house are my rooms. I stand changing clothes. I realize a window is open and I can be seen by two men below. I determine that they will not be allowed to see me unclothed and I move to another part of the room.
>
> I am downstairs at a counter which forms the center—the connector part of the house. I am asking something of the man behind the counter. He is the innkeeper. I move to the other side of the building, to the left, and walk down some wooden stairs into a basement. A dog begins to walk over to me. He is white, wears a collar. He looks like a "shabby" poodle. As he walks to me I question whether he will attack me. I think that because he is the house dog, he must be friendly. I decide that I will not be afraid of him.
>
> The dog comes up two steps and touches my left hand. My fingers are in his mouth. He starts to bite my hand. I look at his teeth and see that he is trying to bite me hard, that he has decided to attack me. I attempt to withdraw my hand, but he holds on really tight.

The above dream is the first part of an extensive three-part segment. It occurred during a residential week of intense daily studies in my doctoral graduate program.

In dream analysis, it is important to identify the conscious life of the dreamer.

What is happening in the waking state that becomes aligned or misaligned with the unconscious in dreams? During that week of study, one group activity occurred that aligned with the above dream in an important way. This will be discussed later in more detail.

The initial dream quality or feel is one of passivity, like waiting to be wakened. This passivity is one aspect of the Shadow in the dream. Others include trust, power, and responsibility. The dreamer does not wish to be seen as suggesting a defensiveness and unwillingness, to be visible—to be seen "unclothed." Within the dream, locations appear important. The house is shaped like an "H," which consists of top/bottom, left/right, and center.

The right is a place of security, "my right-hand man." It is in this place that I secure myself in moving away from the open window. The dog bites my left hand. It is the left that cannot be trusted, evil-sided, and, in my case, the non-preferred hand. It is the feminine side.

I move right to left, passing through the center (where I ask advice), on my way to the "unknown" of the left. It is on the left side of the house that I am bitten by the dog.

My movement in the dreams is also from top to bottom—the movement from the mind to the belly. At the top of the second floor, in my room getting dressed, there is an indication of some attempted modesty or "purity." There is a sense that this is artificial, as in a mask, a persona. There is an energy of hiding even before one is singled out as an object of recognition.

Perhaps the dog does not recognize *me* even though I think of him as the "house" dog. Perhaps the men below do not intend to be voyeurs as I undress. In covering my own body, I have made it impossible to truly know myself. The movement of the dream leads down wooden stops to a basement. In the dream, the steps feel *earthy*. This feeling stands out in contrast to the stripped cleanliness of the rest of the house. As the movement is downward, there is perhaps a quality of shame (abasement) that occurs.

This is a place that has dirt. It is moist and dark. I feel apprehensive as I enter this space.

The color of the dog is white, but he has moved out of dark shadows. Culturally, traditionally, and archetypally, white symbolizes innocence, purity, and trustworthiness. But this is a dog that raises my caution. However, a decision is made to trust the dog because he belongs in the house. In making this decision, I must accept the responsibility for his decision. In the dream, upon placing my hand in the dog's mouth, there is also a decision made in favor of courage rather than fear.

The quality of being lulled to sleep dominates this dream until I move down the stairs to the basement. The dog's attack forces me to respond, to do something. His bite addresses the need for the dreamer to wake up, not to be lulled asleep. In his role as protector of the house, the dog serves to protect the dreamer by waking her up to herself. There are many possible things in the basement. Some of these may be fearful. The dog is there perhaps to awaken the sleeper to the risks that are

86 The Jungian shadow

below. Though the dreamer has been directed by the man at the "center" to go into the basement, the dog serves as guard(ian) in warning that there is a need to be alert. Before going deeper, I must be awake.

One day, after the above dream, I participated in a group process experience with fellow classmates. During this activity, several individuals, whom I had considered friends, criticized and verbally attacked me. The experience was very impactful in my life and served as in indicator of a need for self-examination. In the dream, my dog of aggression has bitten me as if saying, "wake up to your own aggression/assertiveness."

The most significant aspect of the group encounter was what I felt to be the "attack" of classmates. But surrounding this attack, as in the case with the dog, was a subtle feeling of trusting without actual experience—allowing oneself to fall asleep through a false sense of security and trust. Within the group there had been some exploration in friendship building but apparently an inadequate amount. One incident in the group process was a screaming episode where another member of the group and myself screamed at each other in a very angry, aggressive manner.

This experience pointed to my own aggressiveness, perhaps hidden as in the dream under a persona of affability. I was further "pushed" to see this side of myself because of the following dream.

Personal dream

> I am in my house. I am being attacked by gang members. I run to different parts of the house defending myself. I beat them up and overcome each one. Eventually, someone comes that I've been waiting for—a young man. He comes into the house with a young woman.

If it is true that the male in the above dream represents my animus, then he is accompanied by my Shadow in the form of the female. In this dream, it appears that I "overcome" or integrate my aggression, presented as gang members.

This is the first in a series of dreams over an almost 10-year period where I have not run away from the "aggressor." I am not so certain that "defending" is the best state, but at this time it does appear more favorable than running away in fear. There seems to be an alliance between the two aforementioned dreams. It is almost as if the shorter dream, where I am attacking and defensive, prepares me for the next dream. Though the Shadow is present in the gang dream, the young man seems to bring a healing energy through his presence. In a similar way, this same quality exists as I move into the center of the house in the dog dream. But in this dream, my aggression is much more focused in the form of the dog, although still there is movement from passive to aggressive.

Both of the dreams, coupled with my group process experience, indicated the need for me to assess my own aggression, passivity, and responsibility in terms of my relationship with others. It indicated a need to go deeper than the persona, to explore the issue of vulnerability and self-trust and the value of not hiding in relationships through an emotional stance of defensiveness. I could see the value of not hiding. When a member of the process group indicated her fear of me when she wanted to speak her "own mind," I was surprised and insulted. It was very easy at the time for me to see her aggression and her projected fear. In dream analysis, I was able to claim my own and also the part of me that passively lulls myself and perhaps others into a false sense of trust.

Tavistock Jungian group experience

A striking aspect of the summer's group process experience was the topic of race. One man in the group brought it forth as an issue, stating that it was a part of me and present "every time you open your mouth." This individual later repeatedly yelled at me to "shut up," as he did not wish to hear what I was saying to the group. Because he presented race as a component of the experience, I attempted to pursue this topic with him and other group members at later times.

The results ended in what I consider to be a failure. Though race differences and racism continued to be one aspect of the Shadow within my group of school peers, individuals were for the most part unwilling to explore and claim their parts of this Shadow.

If I reverse color symbols in my dream, the white dog is actually not to be trusted. In the African American experience, white represents neither purity nor innocence. A variation on the hand incident is that I should have known better because the dog was white.

Jung's collection of dreams included a very limited number by Africanist people, and yet he felt sufficiently confident to place Africanist people at the bottom of his "scale of consciousness." It is my belief that even the dreams of African Americans differ, because of slavery, from those of African descent who remained on that continent. To use symbols developed by Jung without reviewing his racist Shadow and considering cultural considerations, applying them to Africanist individuals can be less than valuable.

As I review the two dreams presented here, I explored the Shadow in terms of my own cultural experiences as well as in terms of racism. If some part of me believes that white is not to be trusted and that the dog is responsible for me putting my hand in its mouth, when do I become responsible for my own Shadow work? In the gang dream, I am defending, not sitting passively. I am also attacking. I believe that the dog in my dream parallels the yelling male classmate, and that this dream was anticipatory of the group process experience. The dream can be "read" in terms of my own aggression, but because I participate in the collective, does it not also hold the archetypal energy of racism?

How would Jung analyze my dream, an Africanist, in terms of his theories that must conclude that my consciousness was lower and limited to a certain level?

If I interpret Jung's work from the point of view of perhaps a White individual engaged in the work of being a psychoanalyst, most if not all of his basic theories would be acceptable—it has been this way, apparently, for decades. As an African American, I am obligated to investigate, reinterpret, modify, and even reject segments or all of these same theories.

Carrying the Shadow

It is no accident that during the development of the theories of American psychoanalysis, African Americans became the carriers of a sociological White Shadow that has masqueraded as psychology for close to 100 years. There is a strange irony that in "creating" the Shadow of African Americans, Jung identified his own Shadow and that of others like him who chose to define the Shadow, and Africanist people based on racial/racist standards. Shadow, to the observing eye, consists of projections that cannot be tolerated by the subject. Jung says, "It is not the conscious subject but the unconscious which does the projecting. Hence one meets with projections, one does not make them" (CW 9ii, Para. 17). The meeting and carrying of a White imaginative Shadow projected onto African Americans began before American slavery. This Shadow remains today as an intricate part of the American psyche.

The archetype of Shadow, according to Jung, held not only parts of the personal unconscious but also aspects of the collective unconscious. When investigating a dream—with or without associations—there is a possibility of observing aspects of Shadow archetypal energy. However, over time, one is also able to observe characteristics of Shadow projections toward *others*. Jung said of Shadow projections:

> While some traits peculiar to the shadow can be recognized without too much difficulty as one's own personal qualities, in this case both insight and good will be unavailing because the cause of the emotion appears to lie, beyond all possibility of doubt, in the other person.
>
> *(CW 9i, Para. 16)*

Historically, African Americans have "carried" White projections in a variety of areas. Most of these began in Africa and Europe, and all of these projections established the basis for the justification of slavery. The most dominant of these Shadow projections is that Blacks are inferior to Whites. Though this is simply stated, it has been a powerful projection that for centuries validated the start and continuation of American slavery. This idea of Whites being "better" has been the over-arching concept and belief that has ruled American policy in the area of politics, education, and religion for centuries. The idea of a human scale of one being better than another based on ethnicity came from slavers and missionaries and evolved into American consciousness. Robert Guthrie states the following in *Even the Rat Was White*:

> As an outgrowth of explorers' observation and the deductions by some European philosophers, a concept emerged (circa 1730) arguing that although nature is created innocent, all things degenerate when touched by civilization. The idea becomes a double-edged sword in that, while the concept suggests inherent evils of so-called civilization, it labels dark-skinned people as savage thus lending themselves to Eurocentric investigations, measurements, and

studies. The myth of the Noble Savage emerged and moderated somewhat the disapproving European attitudes toward dark-skinned people in general but did not prevent most Europeans from maintaining a view of the African as barbaric and liable for enslavement.

(Guthrie, 2004, p. 8)

It is also possible to state that, in Jungian terms of the concept of *Opposites*, it would be only natural that some "scale" of measurement needed to be created in order to mediate the psychic need for the actual and theoretical development of a theory of Opposites.

Racial inequality proved to be a very strong and steadfast expression of the Opposites. Skin color was an obvious choice for separation of different ethnic groups.

From here, all other "negatives" could be added to the "dark" qualities that existed in those with dark skin. Adding the measurement of "better than" provided Jung, amongst other men during his time, with a way to formulate an Other that could absorb and carry Shadow projections.

A second Shadow project that African Americans have carried over centuries has been one of physical prowess. The most obvious reason for such a projection was the need for African Americans to be the enslaved laborers that were necessary to the American plantation system. It is difficult to imagine that millions of individuals could participate in the slavery system if they had a belief that Africans and later African Americans were physically no more capable than them of being slave labor. The idea that African Americans were "made" for plantations supported the idea of "breeding" for these plantations.

The projection here is that the African American can endure and bear up under the worse of physical conditions because they are actually stronger. However, it is important to note that this strength is not one of intellect; rather, it is only of physical endurance and power. Once again I share Guthrie's words from *Even the Rat Was White*:

> The earliest recorded attempt by American researchers to measure psychological capacities in different races was made in 1881 when C.S. Meyers tested Japanese subjects and proved that the Asians were slower in reaction time than were Europeans. Shortly afterwards, utilizing a popular reaction time device, Bach (1895) tested American Indians and Blacks and *concluded that the "primitive peoples" were highly developed in physiological tasks and attributes* while "higher" human forms "tended less to quickness of response in the automatic sphere; the reflective man is the slower being."
>
> *(Guthrie, 2004, p. 47, italics added)*

It is from these very early beginnings of psychology as a field in the nineteenth century that African Americans were formed consciously and unconsciously into a symbol of Shadow. As the American nineteenth century progressed into the twentieth, an effort was made to reinforce the projection of African Americans, especially men, as strong, and an application that needed to be found for this strength developed following slavery, forcing labor on chain gangs into professional athletics. African American men were to become the gladiators of the American athletic field. However, racism did interfere with this at first. Though Black men were thought and had been "proven" to be strong in physicality, the bias against allowing them to participate in group sports with White athletes meant that they were prohibited from doing so. It was not until 1952, when Jackie Robinson entered major league baseball, that African American men would be allowed to play professional sports with their White peers. However, when we look at sports now, we see the realization of what has been considered a social problem in America—the limits of educational and therefore professional opportunities for African American males. It is uncanny that the early projections of Africanist physical strength over intellectual power continues to live today in the conscious and perhaps unconscious in our society.

Here, I will repeat a section of Jung's quote from earlier in this chapter: "On this lower level with its *uncontrolled or scarcely controlled emotions* one behaves more or less like a primitive, who is not only the passive victim of his affects but also singularly incapable of moral judgment." The emphasis on the words "uncontrolled or scarcely controlled emotions" is mine.

These words speak directly to the Shadow projection that first Africans and then African Americans have been enduring for many decades, certainly through the years of the development of American psychology. One of the most painfully realized creations of the racism embedded in the idea that Africans showed the absence of emotional control was the continuation of this idea in the Blackface stereotypes and other American film images that began to dominate American consciousness at the turn of the twentieth century.

The projection—which became literal as the film industry developed—of African Americans as jovial or weepy, limited in the fullness of emotional range, began with early anthropological and missionary visits to Africa and eventually evolved into a projected belief that African Americans were "happy" and contented working and living on plantations as slaves. This projection of extreme emotionalism in terms of "happiness" was one that very well suited the generational slave trade. However, it was a false narrative. Jung says: "The effect of projection is to isolate the subject from his environment, since instead of a real relation to it there is now only an illusory one" (CW 9i, Para. 17).

Slavers and all those engaged in the actions of slavery and the social and political racist activities that have occurred since those days of slavery were engaged in an illusory story of African American happiness at being the objects of racial discrimination, torture, and abuse. In fact the opposite is true. The authentic feelings of African Americans were more likely ones of deep sadness. This is oftentimes reflected in the "sorrow" songs of slaves.

The projected idea of a White collective Shadow that holds that African Americans were "happy" with their racially imprisoned condition can only be seen as a projection in service of a White subject.

In the *Melancholy of Race: Psychoanalysis, Assimilation and Hidden Grief*, author Ann Anlin Chang says:

> When we turn to the long history of grief and the equally protracted history of physically and emotionally managing that grief on the part of the marginalized, racialized people, we see that there has always been an interaction between melancholy in the vernacular sense of affect, as "sadness" or the "blues", and melancholia in the sense of a structural, identificatory formation predicted on—while being an active negotiation of—the loss of self as legitimacy.
>
> *(Chang, 2000, p. 20)*

Related to this Shadow projection of "happiness" is what Jung terms "moral judgment" and his statement that "primitives" are incapable of having such morality. Jung's belief that those of Africanist ancestry are incapable of moral judgment became another cornerstone for the justification of slavery. The intended purpose of the missionaries sent by European kings and queens was to "save" the souls of African and South American indigenous peoples. This projection of the absence of soul amongst "primitive" people was developed and enhanced for centuries. The idea that Africanist individuals lacked moral judgment in actuality showed the lack of moral judgment on the part of those who became their enslavers. No doubt there were some Christian men who believed that they were "saving" the "heathen," but in the end, after centuries of slavery and its aftermath, including the American Civil War, we understand the immorality of slavery.

We understand that there is no justification for such a catastrophic event to have existed and for as long as it occurred. We would ask ourselves the question, *whose soul needed saving?*

The projection of this Shadow insisting on a lack of morality in the Other—the "primitive"—directly returns to the White Other because "Projections change the world into the replica of one's own unknown face" (CW 9i, Para. 17).

One of the projections carried by African Americans has historically been that we are thieves. As with all of these racially inspired Shadow projections, the carrier holds the truth. We were stolen. We are not the thieves.

The projection of African Americans being thieves lives on today, being most often seen in the discourse among some Americans castigating us as living on welfare, being lifelong wards of the government. This is a legacy of what began as a projection of African Americans as thieves. This falsehood has found its way into American culture and politics.

There are several more ways in which African Americans have carried this racial Shadow for a very long time. These projections, fueled by Black racial complexes, have included at first creating an abnormality regarding what was called *animism*. The spiritual belief dominates amongst many Africans that the vitality of soul existed within all objects. This was at first denigrated by missionaries and other Whites who initially came to Africa. Over time, however, even Jung came to confirm the existence of "life" and movement within what appeared to be inanimate objects.

References

Chang, Anne Anlin. (2000). *The Melancholy of Race: Assimilation and Hidden Grief.* Oxford: Oxford University Press.

Dalal, Farhad. (1988). "Jung: A racist." *British Journal of Psychotherapy*, v. 4, issue 3, pp. 263–279.

Guthrie, R. (2004). *Even the Rat Was White: A Historical View of Psychology.* Boston, MA: Pearson Education.

Jung, C. G. (1993). *Memories, Dreams, Reflections* (13th ed.). New York: Random House.

Perera, Sylvia. (1986). *The Scapegoat Complex: Toward a Mythology of Shadow and Guilt.* Toronto, ON: Inner City Books.

Young-Eisendrath, Polly. (1987). "The absence of Black Americans as Jungian analysts." *The Quadrant Journal*, v. 20, issue 2, pp. 41–53.

8
THE DREAMERS OF SAINT ELIZABETH HOSPITAL

Jung visited America in September 1912, during which time he gave lectures at Johns Hopkins Hospital in Baltimore. One month later, he returned to America at the invitation of psychiatrist Trigant Burrow. Though Freud had declined Burrow's invitation, Jung was eager to revisit the United States because, at the time, he was deeply involved in dream research. He wanted to develop his theories of the collective unconscious and archetypes, and toward that end, he wished to analyze the dreams of African Americans. Jung hoped that his trip would unconditionally confirm one important element of his theory of the collective unconscious: racial heritage was not a determining factor in the creation of archetypal images. In October 1912, Jung traveled to Washington, D.C., where he remained for one month and conducted analysis with 15 African American male patients at St. Elizabeth Hospital. During this time, one of the patients told of dream imagery that Jung believed reflected the Greek myth of Ixion. Jung later stated that this patient's dream validated his own belief in the universality of the archetype (1935/1976, CW 18, Para. 83). Jung made no mention about the culture, other dream symbols, or associations of the African American patients. In reference to this event, Jung states:

> I give you this example of a mythological motif in a dream merely in order to convey to you an idea of the collective unconscious. One single example is of course no conclusive proof. But one cannot very well assume this Negro had studied Greek mythology, and it is improbable that he had seen any representation of Greek mythological figures.
>
> *(1935/1976, CW 18, Para. 82)*

Though Jung states that his example is not conclusive, it is this *single* example that verified his theory of the nonracial aspect of the unconscious. Jung fails to provide us with any opportunity to see more deeply into his own thinking or into the psychology and culture of the dreamer. We are left to wonder about Jung's use of this particular dream image and his own need to substantiate his theory.

Prior to these American visits, Jung had explored his theory of the collective unconscious in his own clinical work with patients at Burgholzli Hospital at the University of Zurich. Regarding his theory at that time, Jung states,

> It is not a question of a specifically racial heredity, but of a universally human characteristic. Nor is it a question of inherited ideas, but of a functional disposition to produce the same, or very similar ideas. This disposition I later called the archetype.
>
> *(1912/1967, CW 5, Para. 154)*

However, Jung later adds, "The archetype is essentially an unconscious content that is altered by becoming conscious and by being perceived, and it takes its colour from the individual consciousness in which it happens to appear" (1934/1968, CW 9i, Para. 6). Yet, because Jung does not provide any associated material of the dreamer, and because he refers to intelligence as a measure in his consideration of the dream, stating, "He was a very uneducated Negro from the South and not particularly intelligent" (1935/1976, CW 18, Para. 81), we are unable to understand the true nature of the dreamer's unconscious material.

In this way, Jung apparently denies the dreamer a capacity for symbolic receptivity and an opportunity for interpretation, which on other occasions he claims must be *defined by the dreamer's individual consciousness*.

Jung has credited a woman patient referred to him by colleague Franz Riklin for strengthening his belief in the archetypal nature of the collective unconscious. He has also said that his experience with this patient was the *turning point* of his understanding of the collective unconscious. In *Symbols of Transformation*, Jung says of this case:

> It concerns a paranoid woman patient who developed the stage of manifest megalomania in the following way: She suddenly saw a strong light, a wind blew upon her, she felt as if her "heart turned over," and from that moment she knew that God had visited her and was in her.
>
> *(1912/1967, CW 5, Para. 154)*

Jung continues, "This remarkable case prompted me to undertake various researches on mentally deranged Negroes" (1912/1967, CW 5, Para. 154). Jung thought that the contents of the unconscious, such as archetypal dreams, were not produced because of a dreamer's race but in spite of any obvious ethnicity. However, Jung needed to prove that this archetypal theory was applicable to non-Europeans. With the support of Trigant Burrow, whom Jung had met in the United States in 1909 and who had followed Jung to Europe as an analysand, Jung made his October 1912 visit to America. It was his opportunity to observe firsthand the archetypal and symbolic thinking and expression of individuals of African descent. He states,

> When I went to America to investigate the unconscious of Negroes I had in mind this particular problem: are these collective patterns racially inherited, or are they "a priori categories of imagination," as two Frenchmen, Hubert and Mauss, quite independently of my own work, have called them. A Negro told me a dream in which occurred the figure of a man crucified on a wheel.
> *(1950/1976, CW 18, Para. 81)*

William Alanson White was an early advocate of American psychoanalysis, a founding publisher of the *Psychoanalytical Review*, and, in 1912, the superintendent of St. Elizabeth Hospital. The first issue of the journal contained a lead article by Jung entitled "The Theory of Psychoanalysis," which continued into the second volume of the *Psychoanalytical Review* in 1915 (D'Amore, 1976). White arranged for Jung to see the 15 African American patients at the hospital. There was some discussion between the two men that St. Elizabeth's might be modeled after Jung's Burgholzli Hospital in Switzerland. White was developing his own ideas concerning the applicability of psychoanalysis to the mentally ill population of St. Elizabeth's.

The hospital medical records of the 15 patients whom Jung saw are unavailable since patient records during that time were sometimes poorly maintained, especially for the mentally ill. The social stigmatization of this population typically meant that family members left complete care of sick patients to sanitariums and hospitals such as St. Elizabeth's (Grob, 1994). Even Trigant Burrow, in a 1910 letter to his mother, demanded she not reveal to anyone that he was working with "insane" patients or visiting them at an asylum during his European stay (Brottman, 2011).

In the early years of American psychology, patient's names were not generally revealed except to those directly involved with patient care, and psychiatrists have traditionally given pseudonyms to patients in order to protect the therapeutic relationship.

Yet these practices don't fully account for Jung's curious lack of attention to personal details and associations of his patient's Ixion dream. It is most puzzling that Jung chose not to elaborate on the details because the Ixion dream was the one dream that *confirmed* a most important aspect of his archetypal theory—the very reason for which he had traveled to America. Jung says of this absence of patient information—the associative details—in his Tavistock II lecture:

> For the moment, I have to content myself with the mere statement that there are mythological patterns in that layer of the unconscious, that it produces contents which cannot be ascribed to the individual and which may even be in strict contradiction to the personal psychology of the dreamer.
> *(1935/1976, CW 18, Para. 83)*

Jung appears to have been satisfied that his theory had been substantiated, and we can only imagine that he was not sufficiently interested to discuss information regarding the "personal psychology of the dreamer." Because we do not have Jung's clinical records, it is not possible to ascertain what, if any, associative dream details he collected at the time of his meeting with the dreamers of St. Elizabeth's Hospital.

Within a few weeks following his visit to America, Jung wrote a letter to Freud telling him of the success of his own theory of libido, tied with the multiplicity of the unconscious, including its sexual nature (McGuire, 1974). Jung also informed Freud that he had completed analysis with 15 patients at St. Elizabeth Hospital. Jung's letter did not discuss his theory of the collective unconscious nor his newly realized acceptance of the nonracial aspect of this theory.

Jung returned to Europe with the belief that he had fulfilled the purpose of his American visit. He states, "I was able to convince myself that the well known motif of Ixion on the sun wheel did in fact occur in the dream of an uneducated Negro" (1956/1976, CW 5, Para. 154). We have to wonder if in his eagerness to substantiate his theory, Jung ruled out the possibility that there were any differences among races pertaining to the collective unconscious, archetypes, and archetypal images. Jung makes no further mention of the 15 patient-dreamers in the *Collected Works*, except for occasional scattered references to the African American Ixion dream.

In his 1935 Tavistock Lecture II, Jung says, "I will not mention the whole dream because it does not matter. It contained of course its personal meaning as well as allusions to impersonal ideas, but I picked out only that one motif" (1935/1976, CW 18, Para. 81). This article gives us the opportunity to return to Jung's investigative work conducted 100 years ago. The passage of time gives us a contemporary perspective from which to explore what Jung believed did "not matter" in 1912 in terms of his theory, African Americans, and cultural consciousness.

Let's turn to the myth of Ixion in order to deepen our understanding of the possibilities inherent in this singular dream. Ixion, the main character of the Greek myth, was the king of a Thessalian tribe, who married Dia and promised a dowry to his father-in-law, Deioneus. Later, however, he refused to pay. In revenge, Deioneus stole Ixion's horses. When Deioneus arrived as a guest at the home of his new son-in-law, Ixion pushed him into a pit of fire.

This act is identified as the first instance of the murder of an invited kinsman in Greek mythology. For this outrageous act, no god would grant Ixion absolution. Finally, Zeus relented and invited Ixion to Olympus. While there, Ixion seduced Hera. When Zeus discovered this, he replaced Hera with the cloud image of Nephele. Ixion mated with her, and from this union, the race of centaurs was born. Enraged, Zeus commanded Hermes to tie Ixion to a wheel of fire from which he could never escape. The wheel spun through the heavens, but according to legend, eventually settled in Tartarus. In addition to the image of the burning wheel, embedded in this myth is psyche's story of the archetypal pattern of guest and kin relationships. When Jung heard the specific description of the St. Elizabeth's patient, to whom I will refer as Dreamer One, he seized upon the single image and connected it to the Greek myth. It seems he did not consider other possible thematic meaning, particularly that of kinship and betrayal, nor did he relate the dream to any other aspect of the myth in relationship to the dreamer or his culture.

Jung states that mythology is a manifestation of the archetypes. He also says that it is impossible to know the meaning of a dream without the associations of the dreamer. We might, then, ask why Jung, though collecting personal unconscious material in the form of a dream, does not provide us with the very information he urges the therapist to gather. Jung states:

> But the objective psyche is something alien even to the conscious mind through which it expresses itself. We are therefore obliged to adopt the method we would use in deciphering a fragmentary text or one containing unknown words: we examine the context. The meaning of the unknown word may become evident when we compare a serious of passages in which it appears. The psychological context of dream-contents consists in the web of associations in which the dream is naturally embedded. Theoretically, we can never know anything in advance about this web, but in practice it is sometimes possible, granted long enough experience.
>
> Even so, careful analysis will never rely too much on technical rules: the danger of deception and suggestion is too great. In the analysis of isolated dreams above all, this kind of knowing in advance and making assumptions on the grounds of practical expectation or general probability is positively wrong. It should therefore be an absolute rule to assume that every dream, and every part of a dream, is unknown at the outset, and to attempt an interpretation only after carefully taking up the context.
>
> *(1936/1968, CW 12, Para. 48)*

From a Jungian interpretive stance, without the dreamer's associations and a context, we are unable to surmise the possible meanings of this dream. Jung informs us that it is archetypal because he has identified a vivid and predominant image of Ixion. It is possible to study many mythological and historical stories and find references to the fiery wheel or the sun wheel, and in that way one might be convinced of the accuracy of Jung's connection of this dream imagery with the archetypal.

In contemplating this dream, it would be interesting to relate its most significant image to that which might be an American—and even more specifically, an African American—cultural consciousness. Jung insists that the wheel of fire appearing to Dreamer One, though he is tied to it, has nothing to do with the cross but is only connected to the myth of Ixion (1935/1976, CW 18, Para. 81). This being true, why could it not *also* be connected and related to the cultural aspects of sacrifice and suffering to which Jung himself refers? In considering the dream image of an African American man early in the twentieth century, could this not have an association to cross burnings and murders perpetrated by the Ku Klux Klan?

Yet, Jung discounts the possibility of other associations by proposing that Dreamer One would have no knowledge of a wheel as source for punishment and that, due to the latter's experience of Christian religion, he would have been more familiar with a cross in connection with sacrifice (1935/1976, CW 18, Para. 1285).

In fact, African Americans were very familiar with many forms of sacrifice, torture, and execution from the earliest days of slavery on the North American continent. The use of the wheel as an instrument of torture or punishment had been in effect since before medieval times, even in European societies. Executions in the United States from the nation's early years frequently involved the torture and death of slave revolt participants by the "broken wheel." This refers to the practice of using a wooden wheel to which the bodies of individuals considered to be criminals were affixed so that their bones could be broken with a hammer or metal tool. This form of torture, popular in the Middle Ages, used large, spoked wheels through which men and women were beaten while the wheel was turned. Death was always a consequence. The wheel was used in New York City in 1712 to punish African Americans following a slave rebellion (Death Penalty Information Center, 2011).

It is very likely that, only 50 years after Lincoln's Emancipation Proclamation, Dreamer One would have known about the punishment of African American men by use of the wooden wheel. Perhaps Dreamer One's images are both archetypal *and* cultural?

When we consider the implications of the dream imagery shared with Jung in 1912, we must question what the consequences of Jung's omitting attention to this cultural layer of the unconscious might be.

With the help of the psyche, personal associations, and cultural references, a dreamer can engage images and work them through for their symbolic meaning. Yet at times, Jung wrote in a way that did not represent African Americans as thinkers with psychological depth. He tells us, "Investigation is complicated by the fact that the Negro does not understand what one wants of him, and besides that is ignorant (does not know age, has no idea of time)" (1935/1976, CW 18, Para. 1285). He states that Dreamer One is "a Negro of not much intelligence" (1935//1976, CW 18, Para. 81). Are there ramifications of this attitude that might still persist? How do we, as Jungian analysts and particularly as American analysts, reconcile this part of Jungian history, being ourselves both products of this legacy and of an ethnically diverse society? I believe that one of the first steps is to create and participate in more conversations and dialogues regarding Jung, Jungian psychology, and African Americans.

The African American dreamers with whom Jung met in 1912 at St. Elizabeth's remain nameless except perhaps to distant relatives. I think of the patient who dreamt of Ixion as Dreamer One because, of all 15 men under Jung's analysis, his is the only partial dream that has survived in Jung's *Collected Works*. Dreamer One is important because his dream survived, even though only in an objectified way.

It is unfortunate that we do not have the text of the dream, and it appears that Jung did not consider his other possible dreams, personal unconscious material, and associations in any further lectures or writings. One might consider Dreamer One as representative of the invisibility of African Americans and their culture in the recorded history of American Jungian psychoanalysis.

Is it possible that this theme of African American invisibility in the development of Jung's theory has influenced us as contemporary Jungians? Is there relevance to the historical invisibility of African American culture and symbols in analytical psychology and in the contemporary practice of Jungian psychology?

African Americans who participated in "scientific" studies and analysis under White American psychologists, psychiatrists, and medical institutions in the early days of psychology often remained nameless (Skloot, 2010). This paper acknowledges the 15 nameless dreamers from St. Elizabeth Hospital. Hopefully, its message will reverberate, helping those of us who are practitioners of Jungian psychology, as well as those who work in the broader field of psychology, to recognize that there is a layer of the collective unconscious that *is* shaped by ethnicity, race, and culture; and furthermore, that this layer of the unconscious includes a positive African American valance.

Each ethnic group that has arrived in America has faced prejudices stemming from its cultural diversity. However, since African Americans are the only major group that arrived as slaves, and because they were a group that could easily be identified because they are people of color, the racism and bias against this particular ethnic group has made assimilation all the more difficult.

Being easily identifiable and so different in appearance from Americans whose origins were Caucasian were factors that invited a tendency to attribute and project biases, the negative, and shadow elements toward African Americans.

It is still very difficult for many to value and respect African American culture and symbols that have evolved from traditional African sources. Frederick Douglass (1845/1986), W. E. B. Du Bois (1903/1994), Melville J. Herskovits (1941/1990), James Baldwin (1963/1993), and Douglas A. Blackmon (2009) among others, have provided us with extensive reflections on the devaluation of and disrespect for African Americans and their cultural heritage.

One particularly interesting example of devaluation is the long and arduous social debate over the relevance of West African linguistic features as important and meaningful to African Americans in terms of Ebonics. Many Americans refused to accept that Africans had a linguistic structure to their language, that this structure was intact in contemporary African American speech patterns, and that it was part of a valuable and positive cultural inheritance (Smitherman, 1977).

Cultural consciousness can be defined as an awareness of those events, people, circumstances, beliefs, and moral attitudes that signify belonging to a particular ethnic group. A positive cultural consciousness means having an awareness of the attributes of one's own cultural heritage and that of others without being predisposed to negative assumptions and projections about what forms this heritage, whether we are speaking of linguistics (Ebonics), food (Soul)—or of music, spiritual beliefs, and other ethnic dynamics.

Positive African American consciousness includes a respectful regard for all aspects of the sociological and historical African American life experience without consistent and predominantly negative bias, particularly as to placement on hierarchal psychological levels of (constructed) intelligence.

Constructed views of intelligence, supported by early proponents of psychology, created a false scale of intelligence whereby African Americans were tested and reportedly found to be lacking the intelligence of Whites. This remains an issue even today in the public school testing and teaching of African American children, where "intelligence" is actually a measure of the quantity of information a child may know and is often culturally biased in favor of White children. African American children have their own culture. Questions related to their culture are not incorporated into these "intelligence" tests.

In moving toward a deeper consideration of Jung's consciousness about African American experience, we might consider Jung's own experiences as he dealt with the issue of Nazism and his alleged support of Hitler's racist politics. At different times, publications have appeared regarding Jung's anti-Semitism (Maidenbaum, 2002). In *C.G. Jung Speaking,* a collection of various interviews with Jung over his lifetime, we see Jung's defense against such a proposition:

> Many Americans asked me what I thought about Hitler and his ideas, in the autumn of 1936, and I always expressed concern for the *future of Europe*. It is not true that I ever admired Hitler. However, in the early years before the power devil finally took the upper hand with Hitler, he brought about many reforms and to a certain extent served the German people constructively. I may have said something of this kind as well as talking of the danger ahead, which I had already written about. If I state an historical fact people immediately jump to the conclusion that that implied admiration! The mockery of it! My whole life work is based on the psychology of the individual, and his responsibility both to himself and his milieu. Mass movements swallow individuals wholesale, and an individual who thus loses his identity has lost his soul.
> (Hull and McGuire, 1977, p. 196)

It seems as if Jung's words here, especially those regarding the psychology of the individual, reflect a contradiction to his views in considering the dreams of the African American men at St. Elizabeth's.

We can see now that cultural consciousness of one's own group, and that of others, means practicing a conscientiousness toward the individual, without prejudice based on race or racial hierarchies. It is likely that Jung's omissions and contradictions, along with the repercussions of America's relationship with racial diversity, influenced the development of Jungian psychology in the United States.

African Americans and trauma

The intergenerational trauma affecting African American men, caused by American slavery, has proven devastating and enduring to his well-being and therefore to the African American family structure. Once again, I consider African American men as part of a group who came to America not as typical immigrants seeking geographical change for their betterment but rather through slavery. Due to how

African Americans entered America, the conditions under which they survived under the yoke of slavery and racism, their experience is radically different than that of other social groups arriving in America. This is the major factor when considering the intergeneration trauma of African Americans. It can never be stated too frequently, as a part of the racial complex that exists in the American psyche is a tendency toward forgetfulness of this fact.

In *Reality Matters: The Shadow of Trauma on African American Subjectivity* (2010), author Janice P. Gump states,

> African American subjectivity is marked by trauma. I use the term broadly, to include the life-disruptive quality denoted by post-traumatic stress as well as the developmental trauma found within the family. The trauma may be explicit and conscious, or unavailable to awareness. It may come from the society at large, as in racist acts of oppression or discrimination, or from the nuclear family. And it may be the result of trauma generationally transmitted. But infusing and determining both intrafamilial and societal traumatic acts is the historical fact of slavery.
>
> (Gump, 2010, p. 48)

The black man has fought to become recognized as a person of value in American society. He has struggled to become an honored individual as a citizen, family member, and worker. I have chosen to consider African American men, rather than the entire group of African Americans, for the focus of this section.

It seems important to select a subgroup from a main group of American "immigrants" to allow for more detail of culturally related circumstances. Due to the fact that there is so much psychological damage in the history of African Americans based on ethnicity, the African American male, and also the female, suffer from what some have called post-traumatic stress syndrome. The repeated efforts of African Americans to escape the despair and suffering caused by slavery has continued—even with the election of an African American president.

African American families suffered a huge crisis and damage for all the years slavery existed and even up until today. The family unit was destroyed through the separation, selling, and "breeding" of African Americans by slaveholders. This legacy still continues to affect the African American family.

The question is: can it be repaired? A secondary question would be how best to accomplish this possible repair? Many individuals such as Martin Luther King, Malcolm X, both notable leaders and others, have been willing to give their lives in support of bettering the life conditions of African Americans.

The Black man has had to endure a great deal. He was often portrayed as a sexual predator against White women. This is the historical view of Black men—they are lusting for White women. This image of the African American male has done much to destroy his image and character as a human being and make him an object and symbol of negative White fantasy. He has oftentimes and continues to be the very real target of racially inspired murder.

Black men in American society were oftentimes lynched because they were thought to be seeking sexual relations with—specifically to rape—White women. This idea of Black men in the role of rapist has not left the Black complex of American society. I think it has only gone underground in the unconscious. It appears that White society has often used the idea of interracial sexual activities as an excuse to commit racial violence against Black men.

The punishment for Black men learning to read and write or for hitting a White man was castration. This severely affected the relationship between Black men and women. The Black man was made impotent by the White man, who could then proceed to rape Black women. What is the fairness or justice in such a societal system?

Today, we still must endure racism in our everyday lives. Slavery has attempted to destroy our families, and the general American belief, held mostly by Whites, is that we do not deserve any reparations for this act of traumatic violence—slavery, which lasted for centuries.

What right did Europeans have to invade and steal Africans? Perhaps only because slavery was already an ancient custom—a part of the human psyche. Is it archetypal, this binding of another through slavery? It was not new to Europeans nor to Africans when Europeans arrived on Africa's shores. Africans themselves engaged in the practice of slavery. However, what made European-style slavery in the Americas so horrendous and vile was that slaves were never able to leave that life. Their families were bred to be objects for slave holders to use to make money. It was always up to the "master" if slaves could have their freedom, but this was rarely given.

The result was the American Civil War. However, this was fought not so much to free slaves but to keep the economic wheels of American society working. Lincoln did not wish to have the American Union divided by the secession of Southern states.

Slavery and the Civil War were both based on using African Americans as objects of economic greed, to gain financial stability for the country—Northern manufacturers needed Southern cotton and political pawns to maintain a unified country.

Author Manning Marable, in *The Black Male: Searching beyond Stereotypes* (2000), discusses how Black men were used by the British in the early days of the American colonies to fight against Native Americans. An example he gives is the fight against the Yemassee tribe in 1715. Black troops led the British and exterminated Native American families. Marable says, "In 1747, the all white South Carolina legislature issued a public vote of gratitude to Black men who in times of war behaved themselves with great faithfulness and courage—in repelling the attack of his majesty's enemies" (p. 251).

By this example given by the author, we can see how from the very beginning of their lives in America, Black men were used in war. The saddest irony is that they should have been fighting beside Native Americans, *not* against them.

Black men have been fighting in American wars created by White men since their arrival in America. First it was against Native Americans, then in the Civil

War, then the Spanish American War, then the Korean War, then Vietnam, then Iraq, and now Afghanistan. Black men, during the Vietnam war, protested, and many refused to go fight other men of color.

This was justified. Black men did not have to go and fight—they could refuse. In the case of the draft, however, during the period of the Vietnam war, Black men had no choice except to go to jail. However, as we look at the brisk business of the current prison system, Black men can wind up there anyway, so why not go there in protest instead of off to kill other people? The men Black men march off to kill are most often other men of color.

Marable discusses Susan B. Anthony as one of the main women of the Suffrage Movement and founder of the American Feminist Movement. These women also said they wanted emancipation for Blacks so that they could have civil rights.

However, according to Marable, after the 15th Amendment passed, giving African American males the right to vote, Anthony turned against Blacks. She stated, "I will cut off this right arm of mine before I will ever work for or demand the ballot for the Negro and not for the white woman" (p. 253). When it came to White women or Black men, the same racism emerged. If they really wanted change for the Black man, Anthony and other crusading women would have supported the Black man. They should have known that because they were White women they had the advantage and would eventually get the vote, whereas this was not a guarantee for Black men.

We understand that the Black man is where he is in society today with many of his educational and economic failures based on his past experiences of a selective American racism. Whereas others—immigrants—are able to enter America and achieve societal successes, this has been and continues to be a major challenge for African American men.

To evaluate this opinion, look at the numbers of them in jail, the numbers not employed, and the numbers of those without a high school education.

In James Spradley's *Conformity and Conflict* (2012), the author says, "Inequality is part of most human interactions. One spouse may dominate another; a child may receive more attention than his or her sibling; the boss's friend may be promoted faster than other employees. But inequality becomes most noticeable when it systematically affects whole classes of people. In its most obvious form, inequality emerges as social stratification" (p. 187).

There are two kinds of social stratification: class and caste. In India, the caste system is one you are born into. There is no interaction between individuals of different caste levels. In the United States, we also use a caste system, but we call it a class system—lower class, working class, upper class. In the United States, we can change our class system. It's up to you if you want to move to a different class. In India, everyone is the same ethnicity. Determining class in America is very different. We are many different ethnicities. Just because someone changes their supposed economic class—especially if they are African American—does not mean that the society at large agrees that they are now members of a different "class." African Americans are still bound by ethnicity in terms of how they are viewed by society at large. In India, where everyone is the same ethnicity, this is not the same issue.

Black men do not automatically achieve an "increase" in their "class" because they change economic status. The wealthiest African American men oftentimes marry White women so that they can achieve a "better" position—as viewed by some, an "increase"—in this "class."

This is almost common knowledge amongst African Americans.

These men are attempting to increase their "class" because many believe that in America, they will always be considered an "under-class" because of their color. Economics isn't the only relevant factor in this situation.

The relationship between African American women and men has been strained and damaged by slavery. The separation of families caused African American couples to distrust, betray, and abandon their partners and children. One of the major social problems still facing African American families is abandonment by Black men. This is an unfortunate situation for many African American individuals—men, women, and children. In the United States, everything is race based. I see it on a daily basis. Black people get treated differently than White people, oftentimes by recent and old immigrants. For example, I can be in line at Dunkin' Donuts. The minute a White person arrives, the cashier rushes me to order, to get rid of me, so that he or she can help the White person. I notice that this is especially true for newly arrived immigrants who have not been living in the United States for any great length of time. It is stressful, and a legacy of slavery and racism, that African Americans who have been in this country for generations continue to be treated as if they are second class citizens by new arrivals to America.

Author Richard Robbins, in *Cultural Anthropology* (2013), says, "Blacks in the United States are more likely to be targeted by the criminal justice system. Proportional to its population, the United States leads the world in prison incarcerations, with some 2.3 million in jail. Within that population, Black men and women outnumber Hispanics by more than 2–1 and Whites by nearly 6–1" (p. 272).

Black men will make babies but they won't take care of them. Is this a statement of fact or fiction? This idea dates back to slavery when the African American family was torn apart. Black men had no responsibility for taking care of their own children. This was the job of the "master" or overseer. It seems that this behavior of not taking care of one's own children has become a part of some Black men's psychology. However, African American men, as slaves, could be killed for learning to read or for trying to improve their lives in any way possible that would allow them to take care of their children. Their lives belonged to the slave holder. It was impossible to take care of their own children because in the slavery system they did not *own* any children. The African American man's children belonged to the slave "master." How has this affected the psyche of African American men in terms of their relationship with their own children? When African American men are criticized for not taking care of their children and seemingly abandoning them, are we also remembering the political and social policies that have laid the groundwork for such behavior? Are we considering the negative effects of slavery?

Today, there are social programs aimed at helping Black men stay connected with their children. This is a good social effort to change consciousness in how Black men can be responsible as fathers and husbands.

Spradley, in *Conformity and Conflict* (2012), quotes from "Mixed Blood," an article written by Jefferson Fish, which raises the question of race. The latter believes there is no such thing as race. Fish says, "Many Americans believe that people can be divided into races. For them, races are biological defined groups. Anthropologists, on the other hand, have long argued that U.S. racial groups are American cultural constructions; they represent the way Americans classify people rather than a genetically determined reality" (p. 217).

I believe that race is a construct created by early missionaries and White explorers to separate different ethnic groups. It helped to serve the purpose of slavery, taking control of the land of non-Whites and indoctrinating "natives" with the "dominant" religion—most often Catholicism. The true fact is that we are all—Black and White—of the same species, the human race. Color as race was promoted as a means to create a hierarchy with Whites at the top and people of color at the bottom. This emerged out of a need for White control of non-Whites as they invaded their land, took their gold, and established the Catholic religion to "save" the "natives." Unfortunately, Jung followed this pattern established by Lévy-Bruhl and others who "explored" Africa.

In "Mixed Blood," the author notes that Brazilians have a racial hierarchy based on physical appearance. As is typical in this kind of social division, the more light-skinned you are, the "better" you are in the eyes of society and the more respectfully you are treated in society. This is also true in America. "Race" matters, and the lighter to White you are, the "better" your life advantages—in every aspect of life, from birth to death. This is the world in which we continue to live.

References

Baldwin, James. (1963/1993). *Notes of a Native Son*. Boston, MA: Beacon Press.
Blackmon, Douglas A. (2009). *Slavery by Another Name: The Re-Enslavement of Black Americans from the Civil War to World War II*. New York: Random House.
Brottman, Mikita. (2011). "Shrinking city." *Style Magazine*. January–February, pp.48–53.
D'Amore, Arcangelo (ed.) (1976). *William Alanson White: The Washington Years 1903–1937*. Washington, DC: U.S. Department of Health, Education and Welfare, Public Health Service.
"Death Penalty Information Center. Executions in the United States. 1808–2002:The ESPY File." http://www.deathpenaltyinfo.org/executions-us-1608-2002-espy-file (accessed 12/1/11).
Douglass, Frederick. (1845/1986). *Life and Times of Frederick Douglass*. New York: Macmillan Publishing.
Du Bois, W. E. B. (1903/1994). *The Souls of Black Folk*. New York: Dover Publications, Inc.
Grob, G. H. (1994). *The Mad Among Us: A History of the Care of America's Mentally Ill*. New York: Free Press.
Gump, Janice P. "Reality matters: The shadow of trauma on African American subjectivity." *Psychoanalytic Psychology*, v.27, issue 1, January 2010, pp. 42–54. http://dx.doi.org/10.1037/a0018639

Herskovits, Melville J. (1941/1990). *The Myth of the Negro Past*. Boston, MA: Beacon Press.
Hull, R. F. C. and William McGuire (eds.). (1977). *C.G. Jung Speaking: Interviews and Encounters*. Princeton, NJ: Princeton University Press.
Jung, C. G. (1977). *The Symbolic Life: Miscellaneous Writings* (*The Collected Works of C. G. Jung*, Vol 18, par. 82). Princeton, NJ: Princeton University Press.
Jung, C. G. (2009). *The Red Book: Liber Novus*. New York: W.W. Norton.
Jung, C. G. (1930/1968). "The complications of American psychology." *Civilization in Transition*. CW 10.
Jung, C. G. (1912/1967). *Symbols of Transformation*. CW 5.
Jung, C. G. (1921/1977). *Psychological Types*. CW 6.
Jung, C. G. (1930/1968). *Civilization in Transition*. CW 10.
Jung, C. G. (1934/1968). *The Archetypes and the Collective Unconscious*. CW 9i.
Maidenbaum, Aryeh (ed.). (2002). "Lingering shadows." In *Jung and the Shadow of Anti-Semitism*. Newbury, MA: Red Wheel Weiser, pp. 87–95.
Marable, Manning. (1994). "The black male: Searching beyond stereotypes." In Richard Majors and Jacob Gordo (eds.), *The American Black Male: His Present Status and His Future*. Chicago, IL: Nelson-Hall Publishers.
McGuire, William (ed.). (1974). *The Freud/Jung Letters: The Correspondence between Sigmund Freud and C.G. Jung*. Princeton, NJ: Princeton University Press.
Robbins, Richard. (2012). *Cultural Anthropology* (6th ed.). Belmont, CA: Wadsworth Publishing.
Skloot, Rebecca. (2010). *The Immortal Life of Henrietta Lacks*. New York: Crown Publishers.
Smitherman, Geneva. (1977). *Talkin and Testifyin: The Language of Black America*. Detroit, MI: Wayne State University Press.
Spradley, James. (2011). *Conformity and Conflict* (14th ed.). New York: Pearson.

9
AFRICAN AMERICAN CULTURAL CONSCIOUSNESS AND THE JUNGIAN COLLECTIVE

This chapter discusses the concept of racism and Jungian language within the broader Jungian collective—analysts, practitioners, and individuals, such as our poets and writers who deal with consciousness in a creative way. I believe that the words we use are very powerful, especially those that are racially derogatory. I also believe that for many decades the Jungian community has, with few exceptions, continued to accept the language of Jungian psychology without consideration of the power of what some of Jung's theories and words mean for individuals of Africanist descent. The shadowed denial of the relevance of these negative words and ideas have, I believe, created a lack of desire on the part of many African Americans to explore anything that is Jungian. The most unfortunate aspect of this is that, as I have previously pointed out, major Jungian concepts were initially founded on African ideological principles. It is also very important to note the lack of words put forth by the Jungian community as a way of a *ritual* cleanings for the decades-old "dirt" of Jung's words thrown onto Africans and African Americans.

Some of the words of the poems in this chapter are from the book of poetry titled *Brutal Imagination* by Cornelius Eady. I believe this poet provides us with a very deep understanding of a racial consciousness affecting us as Africanist individuals. His words tell us the story of what it means to be of African lineage.

In his book *Poetry, Language, Thought*, philosopher Martin Heidegger tells us that *language speaks*. His point of view in the essay "Language" addresses how we think about language. He does this through a poem entitled *A Winter Evening*.

Heidegger's main point: "Mortals speak by responding to language in a two-fold way, receiving and replying. The mortal word speaks by cor-responding in a multiple sense." In his use of the poem, Heidegger shows us the immediacy of language. The poem is written in the present tense. A reading of the poem gives us its focus on this moment in time, even though the poem was written decades ago. When I consider Jung and his writings, I know that his words live and affect how we are and practice as clinicians today because *language speaks*.

The writer bell hooks has written many books dealing with the subject of race. She looks at race on both cultural and personal levels. She oftentimes speaks for a collective that is voiceless and assumes powerlessness in our society. I appreciate the frankness of hook's words. She uses language in a most powerful way to show us her vulnerability as a writer and as a woman who thinks through what deeply disturbs her about American society. She is never afraid to use language to tell us what she really thinks—even when it shows her exposed. This exposure is the landmark of assuming power. The willingness to take a visible stand and speak on topics that potentially antagonize everyone around you. She is as vocal about African Americans taking themselves as victims as she is about the historical lineage left to America by Christopher Columbus. hooks often shares some of her childhood experiences as she does in an essay entitled "Whiteness in the Black Imagination" from her book *Killing Rage: Ending Racism* (1995):

> In the absence of the reality of whiteness, I learned as a child that to be "safe" it was important to recognize the power of whiteness, even to fear it, and to avoid encounter. There was nothing terrifying about the sharing of this knowledge as survival strategy; the terror was made real only when I journeyed from the black side of town to a predominantly white area near my grandmother's house. (p. 45)

In this same text, hooks explores the historical context of the Black gaze—the way in which African Americans were required to lower their eyes in the presence of Whites. She ties it to the way in which a population of individuals was made to become invisible. She proposes that because Whites, in their attitude of power, make Blacks invisible because it serves their interests, Whites themselves believe that they are in fact invisible to Blacks. Whites presuppose that Blacks form no opinions or ideas about them and their centuries-old relationship. hooks repeatedly states that not only do Blacks have opinions and ideas concerning Whites but that they hold a consistent remembrance of terror—realized or anticipated because of their relationship with Whites.

The following words are from Jung's *Memories, Dreams, Reflections* (1961/1993), describing an experience of his trip to Africa in 1925. They relate to a dream Jung had about his barber while visiting America years before:

> An American Negro. In the dream he was holding a tremendous, red hot curling iron to my head, intending to make my hair kinky—that is, to give me Negro hair. I could already feel the painful heat, and awoke with a sense of terror. I took this dream as a warning from the unconscious, it as saying that the primitive was a danger to me. (p. 272)

The "terror" that Jung says he experiences in this dream appears not unlike the terror that hooks says is the experience of African Americans on a daily basis. However, the difference is that Jung was able to leave Africa and return to the safety of Europe. This was and is still not available to Africanist individuals because we cannot leave our skin.

The Multicultural Imagination by Michael Adams (1996) details chapter by chapter issues of racism and Jungian psychology. I have focused on Adams's detailed information in his chapter "Going black, Primitive, Instinctive." In this chapter, Adams discusses language and words that have come to define our perceptions of psychological states in the Jungian community and the psychoanalytical community at large. *Primitive, participation mystique*, and *instinctive* are so frequently used as to have become commonplace in open discussions and writings by those involved in the field of psychology. The fact is that these words originated as a means of comparison between Blacks and Whites with the former considered in a pejorative manner. Their usage has not even begun to touch a deepened enough discussion of the use of these words in a relevant, effective way. I never use the word *primitive* except within a context such as this writing because I consider it a direct, aggressive insult to myself and people of color. The fact that it is scattered throughout Jung's collected works and used extensively in his writings to support his theory of opposites and the collective unconscious (Shadow) makes me eager to see a revamping of psychological language because language *does* speak. My question is how many more decades will Jungian analysts, and others in the field of psychology, use such derogatory, racist language and consider it to be normal and inoffensive?

I will repeat here a segment of my dream from Chapter 7:

> The dog comes up two steps and touches my left hand. My fingers are in his mouth. He starts biting my hand. I look at his teeth and see that he is trying to bite me hard, that he has decided to attack me. I attempt to withdraw my hand, but he holds on really tight.

If I go along James Hillman's archetypal lines, I must indicate a specific color of white, remembering that white wants to be "supreme." Archetypally, this is the only position it is capable of holding. According to Hillman, even Blacks acknowledge this when considered on an archetypal level. Doing this, I remember the dog as pure white, snow white, before the dirt of city life lays upon it. If I consider my ethnic heritage, I was wrong to have trusted that the white dog would not bite me. Jungian psychology would say that the bite has awakened me ... my instincts are alive. One other perspective—my aggression, regardless of dog color? Is my aggression fed and fueled by the factor of a white dog? Is the white dog just different, or do opposites, me Africanist and him white, really matter? I believe that these are questions that do matter not only for the interpretation of my dream but also for the broader work that we do with others in dream analysis.

bell hooks again, in her essay "White in the Black Imagination," states:

> If the mask of whiteness, the pretense, represents it as always benign, benevolent, then what this representation obscures is the representation of danger, the sense of threat.

> During the period of racial apartheid, still known by many folks as Jim Crow, it was more difficult for Black people to internalize this pretense; it was hard for us not to know that the shapes under white sheets had a mission to threaten, to terrorize.
>
> That representation of whiteness, and its association with innocence, which engulfed and murdered Emmett Till, was a sign; it was meant to torture with the reminder of possible future terror.
>
> (hooks, 1995, p. 45)

Emmett Till, a teenager who was visiting family members in Mississippi in the summer of 1955, had been accused of "flirting" with a young White woman. In order to protect the *white innocence* of this woman, Till was tortured and murdered by the woman's husband and her brother. The fact that the jury found these men "innocent" served as a "reminder" that "possible future terror" was always a possibility for African Americans. They could be murdered with impunity, even when they were legally innocent, while Whites would avoid justice. Southern law did not protect African Americans.

In "Notes on White Supremacy," Hillman says that we have mixed up archetypal psychology with political psychology. It would be wonderful to sort through into a place of absolute clarity and continuously remain on this path. But we know the unconscious is not like that. We are always challenged by the incongruities of dreams, fantasies ... whatever the imagination can produce. When we include race, racial matters, I believe the adding of this ingredient brings with it passion—even though it may be sublimated.

Susan Smith was a White woman living in South Carolina several years ago who claimed that a Black man had stolen her two children. Eventually, the police were able to determine that she was lying and that she had created a *false* Black man, a character whom she blamed for the kidnapping. She had actually driven her car with her two young children to their deaths in a lake. Cornelius Eady wrote a series of poems recounting the voice and person of the Black man with others involved in the case. Eady writes:, "Susan Smith has invented me to do what nobody else in town will do, what she needs me to do … her need part mythical, Everything she says about me is true."

In the psychologically disturbed state of this mother, she has chosen an African American man to be the murderer of her children. What does this say about the enormous projection of the negative Shadow onto African American men in this society? Eady's poem only reflects what we actually live.

Hillman in *The Dream and The Underworld*, in my opinion, does little better than Jung in his consideration of Africanists in dreams. At the time of this writing, 1979, Hillman says, "it is Jungian convention to take these blacks as shadows, a convention to which there can be no objection." Hillman goes on to identify the Africanist man as Thanatos. He says, "I think it would be archetypally more correct, and so more psychological, to consider black persons in dreams in terms of their resemblance with this underworld context…. In other words their terrifying aspect might be where their true dynamic lies … they present death, the repressed is death. And death dignifies them."

Hillman has done what he has accused others of doing; he has cloaked Africanist people in the same Shadow of Whites sociologically, only this time with what he calls "the idea of a subtle essence." I assume this is his way of making them more archetypal. However, I will add that, over the years, Hillman has written more material that has shown a change in his perspective on Africanist individuals. I appreciate him and his later writings as he attempts to work through creating a post-Jungian dialogue regarding American racial complexes and the archetypal. Time allowed him the ability to accomplish this and perhaps, over time, there will be more of the possibility of a revisionist application to Jung's writing as well.

Many Africanist people agree to let Whites say whatever they want because there is a cultural Africanist assumption that they will lie and make up stories about the African Diaspora to suit their need for power and privilege. Women such as bell hooks, Toni Morrison, and several others use words to illustrate the pathology of these made-up stories.

Psychic imagination, as it relates to African Americans and Caucasians, the archetypal colors of White and Black, always wind up in the arena of culture. I believe this is because the cultural psyche does influence our individual psyches in a movement of exchange. In this same way, I also believe we will always have racism because archetypally there must always be a victim and a persecutor. We must always create an Other to maintain strength within our own ego. I believe *this* to be archetypal. Having ego strength is something Jungian psychology advocates. Differentiation must happen because we do need to be able to take care of our individual selves. However, I also believe that the greater and wiser good is to hold gently the differences that exist between us.

I quote Adams from his chapter "The Color Complex" in *The Multicultural Imagination*:

> The white ego is a white ethic of discipline, restraint, control. I do not mean that whites are, in actuality, more disciplined, restrained and controlled than blacks. What I mean is that in order to sustain this ethic as an ideal the white self requires a black other: if the black other did not exist, the white self would have to invent. Racism or colorism is such an intractable problem because the very persistence of the white ego is dependent on the maintenance of a color complex that enable whites to define the "self" in opposition to an "other". In this sense, blacks function as an effigy of all those "primitive" capacities that whites believe they have relinquished in an effort to become "civilized."
>
> (Adams, 1996, p. 139)

In "Haiti, or the Psychology of Black," Hillman speaks about the seduction of black. He asks the question, what does black intend to achieve? I think it is very important to have a baseline of the definition of archetypal black within the context of a class addressing sociocultural factors.

I find it necessary to remember what archetypal black means without attachment to ethnicity. I believe it is one way we can progress from the projection of black—with all of its embedded meanings—onto people of African descent. Hillman reminds me by his words in this article what I instinctively know. He says,

> The disdain for black is not only contemporary, Western and English. The color black in the Greek world and in African languages also, carried meanings contrasting with white and red and included not only the fertility of the earth and the mystery of the underworld, but also disease, suffering, labor, sorcery and bad luck.
>
> (Hillman, 1997, p. 4)

Hillman, in this article, as have others elsewhere, explained that the word *black* was placed on African people upon the arrival of English-speaking sailors in the fifteenth century. He says, "The English term 'white' to characterize an ethnic group first occurs in 1604, after the perception of Africans as 'black' … White as a term for Christians became firmly established by 1680 in the American language." He states that "Northern European and American racism may have begun in the moralization of color terms." If this is true, then my interest in making clear definitions and origins of psychological words has importance because language speaks.

Last week in session, Diane spoke about her frustration and despair regarding getting the work she would like to obtain as a talented actor. In speaking about herself as an African American, she said, 'black people are victims … we have a slave mentality. They think Obama is going to do something … he is only one person. What he does, doesn't affect me. I'm still on my own."

My patient is alone, despairing, feeling that her talent goes unnoticed. She is in a *nigredo* stage. She also happens to belong to an ethnic group that has been labeled "Black." It will be a part of our work together to help her sort through the parts of herself where she feels race and sex are factors in her inability to be get work as an actor. These dialogues will be unavoidable because she is African American, and her dark state may partly be a result of what she believes is generalized racial discrimination.

Jungian and psychoanalytical writers on racism

In 1987, Polly Young-Eisendrath wrote an article for *The Quadrant Journal* entitled "The Absence of Black Americans as Jungian Analysts." I will share with you more of Young-Eisendrath's ideas in the remainder of this chapter.

I once sat listening at a public forum event as John Gosling, another Jungian analyst, responded to my question regarding Africanist people not becoming Jungian analysts. Did he have any indication as to why this was, since he had lived in America and was a practicing Jungian analyst in his native South Africa? He said that there was an absence of Jungians of African descent, not just in America but around the world.

The way he said these words brought a certain sadness to me. The richness of Jungian and archetypal psychology of which so much comes from Africa was not being realized by individuals of this ethnic lineage.

Twenty-nine years have passed since Young-Eisendrath wrote her article. It has been seven years since Gosling stood that evening and said, "around the world." We might think that things have changed. They have in some ways but certainly not in this respect. The C. G. Jung New York Institute has graduated one other woman of African descent—Celestine Smith. This was in 1964. No other Jung Institute has had an African American female Jungian analyst graduate.

What does this say about Jungian training programs, the American Jungian psychology culture? What does it say about how Jungian language, with all of its racial nuances and overtones, its condemnation of African Americans and Africans within its training programs and teaching materials?

This negative influence has supported the development of the absence of an *entire* ethnic group from participation in Jungian psychology. Gosling stated that traditional healers in South Africa refuse to work with them in doing healing work. He states that they, the Jungians there, have made overtures in this direction. I assume a deep lack of trust on the part of the South African traditional healers. In America, I assume this lack of trust. Racism is imbedded in American institutions. Jungian training institutions are no different, and a problem is the general lack of motivation toward making a change in acknowledgment of the mixed ethnicity of our American society. I believe that psychology training institutes, training men and women to become psychoanalysts, would be the first American institutions motivated to move forward to eradicate racist teachings, revise racist literature, and speak up against previous racist policies.

I believe there needs to be an increase in self-reflection on the part of the Jungian collective and a demonstrated effort at deconstructing the Euro-centric psychological language that alienates African Americans. *Language speaks.* Unfortunately, oftentimes Jungian psychology can only respond to the sound of the qualities of archetypal black equated to the very human, African American.

Several Jungian analysts from communities outside of the United States have put their attention on the issue of racism in Jungian psychology.

I have already mentioned Farhad Dalal, whose article "Jung: A Racist" came ten years following Young-Eisendrath's article on the lack of American Jungian analysts.

Andrew Samuels is a training analyst with the Society of Analytical Psychology in London. His book *The Political Psyche* is one of his works in which he engages in a conversation about racism in the chapter "Jung, Anti-Semitism and the Nazis." Though there is much more said in the chapter about Jung and his relationship with Jews, Samuels does offer the following in terms of African Americans:

> But it is clear that something goes very wrong with Jung's thought when he goes beyond the boundaries of psychology into what has been termed racial typology. When Jung's African stays an imaginal African, the African of dreams, or when Jung studies African myth, he makes a creative though politically limited contribution to social thought. But when Jung generalizes about African character, and does so from a solely psychological point of view, ignoring economic, social, political and historical factors, then he spoils his own work, inviting the severe criticism he has received.
>
> (Samuels, 1993, p. 309–310)

Dalal, in his article, addressed several issues for which Jung was thought to have been racist, in regards to those of African descent. The author begins by stating the two spheres within psychology that are the rationalizations for a racial hierarchy—intelligence quotient (IQ) and the "psychodynamic notion of psyche." Dalal continues to build a case in supporting how we can and must re-think Jungian psychology due to the racist nature of its theoretical foundation. The author states that this foundation is composed of three main equations:

1. The modern Black with the prehistoric human;
2. The modern Black conscious with the White conscious;
3. The modern Black with the White child.

Dalal continues, "It is this which constitutes the core of Jungian Psychology and on which all else is based. The equations are where he begins; these are the beliefs and ideas which he accepts without question." Dalal writes clearly using Jung's words, as the former says he will show how Jung is racist through his theory of "primitive psychology."

A more recent writing regarding Jung and racism by British Jungian analyst Helen Morgan, "Issues of Race in Psychoanalytic Psychotherapy: Whose Problem Is It Anyway?" discusses the racism that seems apparent in the British analytic organizations of which she is a member and within the training of this same institute.

Morgan notes several of the issues I have pointed to in my writing: she speaks of the invisibility of the problem of racism within the analytical institute as a color-blindness; she notes that Black trainees are not encouraged to speak about their feelings about being Black or acknowledge any cultural differences involving race. I quote here from her paper:

> The difficulties they reported painted a picture of the black individual accepted into the training as long as they put aside and ignore their 'blackness'. The pressures were subtle but wearing. Some felt that their ethnicity attracted negative special attention during the interview process, citing instances of being quizzed on matters the equivalent of which were not put to White applicants. Some reported raising points in seminars about theoretical and clinical material from the point of view of diversity, racial difference, cultural variation, racism etc. which were ignored or dismissed by teachers and peers who were clearly uncomfortable in speaking freely about such matters. Generally the climate was one of colour-blindness where trainers, supervisors and analysts took the position that differences in colour are not relevant as we are all the same. This meant a failure to acknowledge any matter of difference and required the black trainee to ignore important aspects of her or his experience.
>
> *(Morgan, 2008, p. 35)*

In a later section entitled "The Analytic Profession," Morgan speaks regarding the topic of race within the profession. She says that there was no literature on clinical experiences where race or racism was a factor, except those written by a few Black psychotherapists. Here is what Morgan says she observes:

> I started researching the matter of how differences in race', colour and culture might affect the work of supervision, and was interested to note that I could find no mention of the topic in the books I read on supervision in psychoanalytic or Jungian analytic psychotherapy.
>
> *(Morgan, 2008, p. 8)*

In writing further, Morgan says:

> This is in stark contrast to the modern texts on supervision in counselling and social work where at least one chapter on the issue seems always to be included. However, on reading some of those chapters in the counselling supervision books I found the majority to take a position of cultural relativism and, in my view, fail to address how the dynamics of 'race' and racism can be thought about from the perspective of the internal world of the psyche. It seemed that the deeper the analytic enterprise, the less the subject is considered of relevance until it is ignored completely in the analytic texts.
>
> *(Morgan, 2008, p. 46–47)*

The ability to ignore, make invisible issues, problems, facts having to do with racism, I consider to be an ongoing problem in American Jungian training institutes. Author Joel Kovel, whom Morgan quotes, appears to believe that white racism is part of social, psychological, and historical patterns. He proposes that we cannot help but be racist because it is a part of our natural inheritance as human beings:

> I return to Kovel's word *saturate*, which is a good one for the way in which racism has penetrated every corner of the society into which we are all born. There is no position one can take that is outside it. If we acknowledge the racist backdrop to our world, then we also have to recognize the particular prejudicial veil that is the inheritance of all White members of this society. The veil may well be one of cordiality but it has guilt, shame, and envy woven into it, complicated as it is by the hatred of the internal racist conversations about the reality of the external and the internal divides caused by racism. Yet, only by finding ways of talking to each other can we gain knowledge of and develop relationship with the other and with ourselves.
>
> It is fear of such shame that freezes our curiosity about each other and prevents us from having ordinary conversations about the reality of the external and the internal divides caused by racism. Yet, only by finding ways of talking to each other can we gain knowledge of and develop relationship with the other and with ourselves.
>
> *(Morgan, 2008, p. 46–47)*

Morgan's writing is very informative and interesting, not only because it absolutely mirrors in many ways my own analytical training experiences but also because her experiences and those with whom she works are across the Atlantic Ocean in England. She addresses the multiculturalism of London and wonders how the absence of Black analytical psychotherapists can exist in such large measure.

Other writers who have noticed and addressed the issue of racism within the psychoanalytical field include Neil Altman, a New York City psychoanalyst, and Barbara Fletchman Smith from London. *Transcending the Legacies of Slavery: A Psychoanalytic View* provides a detailed description of the psychological work that Smith does with her patients who are of Caribbean descent. The issues she presents include the depressed, exhausted mother, the entirely absent father, the emotional impoverishment of relationships due to what the author feels are the residual impacts of slavery.

Smith relates the story of one of her patients by the name of Beth. Beth is a third-generation Caribbean daughter of a mother and grandmother who both eventually returned to the Caribbean. It is noted how Beth's mother was always working very hard, was extremely busy, and was basically unavailable to Beth and her siblings. Her mother was working to be able to purchase a home in the West Indies. When she was finally able to do this, Beth was already traumatized by her current life, which now included the abandonment of her mother, the loss of her intimate partner of 19 years, and her son leaving her home. In addition, she had just lost her job. Smith says, "Beth faced the world feeling totally abandoned yet with a story of her mother having acted reasonably; of her mother having deserved a good life in the sun. She was also seething with a rage of which she was not aware. It was this rage turned inwards that contributed to her serious depression" (2011, p. 41).

Smith writes about Beth noting the absence of a "good enough internal mother," but she also sees how "Slavery created anxieties for women and children that they go on trying to resolve. Women left largely unprotected by men in the past struggle with a conviction that men cannot be relied upon" (2011, p. 42).

Smith's book is powerful for the perspective it provides on the issues of slavery which have affected and continue to affect the psychological health of Caribbean individuals of color. The stories of her patients are similar to my own in temperament and perhaps in the unawareness of how the past trauma of slavery has created an archetypal psychic present that dominates the current life.

Neil Altman's book *The Analyst in the Inner City* provides an introductory paragraph in the first chapter that addresses the entirety of his book.

> Life in the inner city entails a greater burden of stress, loss, and trauma than life in working-class-and-up communities. These conditions predispose to psychopathy (Brown and Harris, 1978) and complications in parenting young children (Halpern, 1993) and form part of what is enacted and experienced in the transference and countertransference when one works psychoanalytically with inner-city patients.
>
> *(Altman, 2010, p. 3)*

Altman provides an in-depth look at his analytical practice within the context of a community clinic and his private practice. He shows his insight into his understanding of racism from the perspective of a White analyst working with African American patients. He is knowledgeable about families, their economic status, and the nuances of psychoanalytical history, theories, and shortcoming as related to African Americans.

Altman gives this reasonable advice:

> My intention has been to argue that it is crucial for the analyst to attempt to become familiar with his or her own racial attitudes and feelings, including racism, in the countertransference.... Although I wish an end to racism were possible, I believe that, given the present state of society and the human psyche, it should be taken for granted that none of us will be able to overcome our personal racist attitudes altogether. Thus, I am advocating that clinicians become familiar with their racism, not that they overcome their racist feelings and attitudes.... As with countertransference in general, no sooner do we deal with one of its manifestations than another appears from the unlikeliest quarter. If it were not so, the analyst's unconscious would have disappeared. Psychoanalysis, in the version that most appeals to me, teaches that no one's unconscious, including the best analyzed analyst's, will ever disappear. Racism, then, will not be dealt by any finite list of its manifestations against which we can attempt to immunize or guard ourselves. It is better that we take the attitude that racism is always there and that vigilance is always required.
>
> *(Altman, 2010, p. 148)*

Thomas Singer and Samuel Kimbles are both Jungian analysts of the San Francisco Jung Institute. The former served as editor of a collection of essays *The Vision Thing*, in which Kimbles had a paper entitled, "The Cultural Complex and the Myth of Invisibility." An evolution from the article is Kimbles's *Phantom Narratives*, published in 2014.

In his introduction to *The Vision Thing*, Singer gives the reader a personal account to what brought him to collect visionary articles for his book. He asks a question and provides an answer about the book:

> What is the collective unconscious brewing up for us as a way of finding meaning in the twenty-first century? This book is a grand tour in time and space of myth and politics in the world as seen through the psyche's eyes of "the one and the many." In these essays, bits and pieces of recombinant visionary myths and political realities can be seen to scatter the landscape of the so-called "global village" like so many shards of Kiefer's Breaking of the Vessels. Thoughtful inspection of these shards reveals a recurrent tension between diversity/disintegration and integration/homogenization. The most optimistic vision for the twenty-first century would be a synthesis of the positive aspect of the "many" (diversity) with the positive aspect of the "one" (integration).
>
> *(Singer, 2000, p. 17)*

Singer is known for his work on the cultural complex following the lead of Joseph Henderson who initiated the first Jungian American focus on the cultural unconscious. It is from this work that Samuel Kimbles's text *Phantom Narratives: The Unseen Contributions of Culture to Psyche* broadens the focus on the cultural collective. This terminology is used extensively by Kimbles and supports the reader in a deeper understanding of how these cultural complexes exist and their influences. Kimbles, an African American, by sharing his own personal dreams, allows the reader to see into the nature of how these particular complexes work. In quoting Bion, Kimbles states: "Bion points to one of my essential points—that cultural complexes cannot be understood within individual psychological functioning alone. They are group-level phenomena and are always an expression of a both/and dynamic—that is, group and individual" (2014, p.10).

Black Issues in the Therapeutic Process by Isha Mckenzie Mavinga (2009) provides details of the training issues that arise for Black psychotherapists in England. The text also addresses issues of trauma and stress that become evident with Black clients during the course of treatment. Through use of the interview format, Mckenzie-Mavinga shows the ideas held by patients, other clinicians who work with Caribbean patients and questions of trainees, such as, what kind of Black Western archetypes are there?

Edward Bruce Bynum is the author of *The African Unconscious: Roots of Ancient Mysticism and Modern Psychology*. It is a book that details the importance of recognizing the beginning of all cultures—which began on the African continent. Throughout the text, Bynum presents fact after fact that support the intellectual, creative, and artistic power that was present in African societies long before the emergence of Greek culture. Bynum says,

> When the genius of Kemetic Egyptian civilization was discovered by Europe in the 18th and 19th centuries, this threatened return of the repressed was handled differently. Egypt was mentally and "scientifically" taken out of Africa and made an extension of European and Middle Eastern history and development. It became "Egypt *and* Africa." ... The indigenous African was erased from the teaching of history and unfoldment of human civilization. This subtle psychological process continues to this day on a large scale.
>
> With a few notable exceptions, in the Eurocentric tradition it was simply inconceivable that highly evolved civilization that gave light to the mind could have its genesis in a dark mysterious world and then move in an African migration down toward the Mediterranean. This is despite the fact that the Romans did not come until Caesar, around 30 B.C.E., that the Greeks did not come in mass numbers before Alexander in 333 B.C.E., that the Jews did not come to be known before Abraham and Joseph, that the Assyrians, Phoenicians, and many other did not come until very late in the day.
>
> *(Bynum, 2012, p. 80)*

Each one of the above authors provides a unique perspective on racism within the area of psychoanalysis. Their voices take us from the interiority of their own personal psychological spaces to the early periods of human existence, documenting the significance of Africa, and into the workings of Jung's theories. It is important to review their writings because it helps to give us a perspective on how far depth psychology has evolved, where it has evolved from, and how far we might have to go—as Singer's writing suggests—in thinking about a vision for the journey.

I will close this chapter with a few thoughts from Polly Young-Eisendrath, whose lone voice was attempting to get others to hear, back in those days when those practicing American Jungian psychologists seemed to suffer from *color blindness* and were unable to hear how times were changing. It appears that in many ways, her words are as true today as they were 30 years ago. I will add my own narrative voice to hers in a *call and response* that intertwines the opposites and provides reflection on how we can be thoughtfully together as American Jungians.

1. "Racism is a psychological complex organized around the archetype of Opposites, the splitting of experience into Good and Bad, White and Black.... The complex of racism usually contains ideas and feelings of power, difference, control and dominance." (Young-Eisendrath, 1987, pp. 41–53)

Young-Eisendrath's idea reflects one of the core features of Jungian psychology. As a central element, it worked very well for Jung to establish understanding of how the psyche works and how we participate in the unconscious and it in us. However, the move toward what brings the concept toward racism is the establishment of a sociological stance of recognizing differences—White and Black—and making one "better" than another.

Clearly, power, control, and dominance are easily established by the way in which Americans have constructed "race" and racial relations. One needed to be over the other. Slavery created a pattern that, I believe, continues today on both the conscious and unconscious levels in our psyche.

2. "The subject of racist feelings and assumptions is dependent on the object of her/his racism because it is the Other that defines the essence of self as Good; through the defensive desire to oppose and devalue that Other, the subject contains the ideal of the Good." (Young-Eisendrath, 1987, p. 42)

I do not think that anyone would argue that those in defense of the "goodness" of white—whether the archetypal white or as projected onto ethnicity of Other—will deny that the Other—black/opposite—does not become devalued. The purpose, conscious or not, is to diminish the other in service of building a stronger ego. It was an absolute necessity in continuing racist political and social policies, to maintain a balance in the society and in American ideals that supported a morally "good" self, the society required a "bad" Other. African Americans easily became that bad Other, not only in an idealized American state of mind but also as reflected in society.

3. "Drawing on Melanie Klein's contributions to object relations theory.... In a primitive splitting and early differentiation, the Other is experienced both as powerfully good and resourceful and powerfully bad and destructive. These two conditions are archetypal—infused with emotion and experienced as separate images (the Great Mother and the Terrible Mother). Both envy and hate are natural states of aggression in early life ... when we interpret the image of a Black person to represent the negative side of the split within our own subjectivity, then we are acting with an unconscious (or conscious) hatred." (Young-Eisendrath, 1987, p. 43)

The inherent contradiction of holding both good and bad can be seen in the way in which Africans came to be used and functioned within American society. The projection of "bad" was made in order to claim them as slaves. Missionaries were abundantly helpful in this way.

As "bad objects," Africans needed to be saved. Slavery became this salvation. In the Americas, slavery continued to serve as the justification for redemption of African souls. The "good" of the African and later the African American was that they contributed to the building of the American economy. African Americans held both the good and bad—the projection of wickedness and the "religious" saving of their souls through European religion. The acts of aggression carried out against Africans, and later African Americans, shows the active hatred in which they were held for centuries.

4. "Blackness in European culture—When we indulge our European parental complexes, we may forget the meaning of such symbolizing: it is a map of what is repressed and denied in the Caucasian psyche. The meaning of blackness is imagined, constructed or created within the mainstream of Caucasian European culture, not within the mainstream of indigenously black or non-white societies." (Young-Eisendrath, 1987, p. 44)

The creation of an African American identity by Whites has been ongoing since the beginning of slavery. The movement from "savages" to be saved historically moved to a sociological construct that was invented. African Americans were encouraged to define themselves. The power of labeling and creating an identity was held by others who imagined people of color to suit their fantasies based on need. This occurred within the field of psychology as well as elsewhere in American society. In Jungian psychology, the Other served well as an opposite with all of the characteristics necessary to enhance the intelligence, worthiness, and value of European culture.

African Americans did not construct an "Other" of less value, as did White Americans.

5. "Envy is a desire to destroy what is seen as powerfully resourceful, but under the control of the Other ... by merging descriptions of sexual abandonment,

African American cultural consciousness

freely expressed joviality and laughter and fantasized connection with sensuality of all sorts, with images of black people ... white readers imagine such resources as outside of themselves. Envy unconsciously leads to fantasies of the possession and destruction of the body of the envied other. Our envy has functioned, I believe to permit our contempt for certain American traits about which Jung was critical ... Jung identifies American qualities of coarseness, childlike directness and noisiness in a way that seems embarrassing in light of European civility. These qualities he links especially to the influence of 'primitives' on the white American psyche. By splitting off these characteristics from ourselves, by denying our white American power-mongering rebelliousness, we protect ourselves from taking charge of our psychology in its non-European social, racial and ideological concerns." (Young-Eisendrath, 1987, pp. 44–45)

Over decades, even through the vaudeville era, with Whites in blackface, imitation of African Americans by Whites made them carry the "childlike directness and noisiness," the joviality, that was always a constructed part of African Americans in the White imagination. Early American White culture chose to show the "fun" and carefree side of African Americans from the beginning—for example, the plantation days of "happy" slaves singing and dancing after working from sun up to sundown in cotton fields. The dancing and laughter with which Jung characterized African Americans was typical of the animated happiness projected onto African Americans. There was rarely a place for acceptance or understanding the harsh reality of slavery or the aftermath of an enslaved life.

6. In Jungian circles, Africans and Black Americans are known mostly as symbols, stereotypes and aspects of ourselves. This is not a moral condemnation, but a recognition of the lack of valid subjectivity other Black American has within our societies." (Young-Eisendrath, 1987, p. 50)

In Jungian circles, as African Americans and Africans are kept as symbols, there is an inability for any meaningful relationship to develop. This is a duplication of the historical idea of African Americans as an extension "object" of subject. African Americans, by their lack of being "special" and being outside the "dominant" group, represent only a part of the White "sub" culture, continuing to live in Jungian thought as outside the homogeneity of Jungian psychology. This type of exclusion translates into an elimination of the possibility of African Americans ever becoming deeply involved in the field of Jungian psychology. The other aspect is, as Young-Eisendrath indicated, how can there be a development of American Jungians? Due to the multiculturalism of America, how can those who practice Jungian psychology think that they can remain "special" without an eventual integration of all people of color in America?

7. "Our silencing of black Americans and our refusal to speak about our own racism betray a kind of fraudulence. I have personally felt a great deal of guilt about my divided loyalties as an American with a social conscience and a Jungian analyst ... Because I live in a society of diversity, and of dominance by the few, I believe that I have a responsibility to articulate a psychology that is relevant to understanding the effects of ethnic, racial and class differences on personal being." (Young-Eisendrath, 1987, pp. 51–52)

It is crucial that the issue of race, gender, and class be a part of open discussion in all aspects of American life, including Jungian psychology.

The silence of Jungian Americans discussing their own particular brand of racism has persisted for close to 100 years. Very, very few have opened their mouths to speak about the inherent racial quality of some Jungian theories. Jung realized and acknowledged racial complexes. His American followers appear to have developed blinders so that they would not see the importance of race, gender, and class in our society. Ignoring racism and racial relations have not made these disappear. They only go underground and emerge as experiences in a collective with immense racial conflict and trauma.

References

Adams, Michael V. (1996). *The Multicultural Imagination: "Race," Color and the Unconscious*. New York: Routledge.

Altman, Neil. (2010). *The Analyst in the Inner City: Race, Class and Culture Through a Psychoanalytic Lens* (2nd ed.). New York: Routledge.

Bynum, Edward Bruce. (2012). *The African Unconscious: Roots of Ancient Mysticism and Modern Psychology*. New York: Cosimo Books.

Dalal, Farhad. (1988). "Jung: A racist." *British Journal of Psychotherapy*, v. 4, issue 3, pp. 263–279. Oxford: Blackwell Publishing.

Eady, Cornelius. (2001). *Brutal Imagination*. New York: Putnam.

Fletchman Smith, Barbara. (2011). *Transcending the Legacies of Slavery: A Psychoanalytic View*. London: Karnac Books, Ltd.

Heidegger, Martin. (2001). *Poetry, Language, Thought*. New York: HarperCollins.

Hillman, James. (1979). *The Dream and the Underworld*. New York: Harper & Row.

Hillman, James. (1986). "Notes on White supremacy." *Spring 1986*. Dallas, TX: Spring Publications.

Hillman, James. (1997). "The seduction of Black." *Spring 61: A Journal of Archetype and Culture*, pp. 1–15.

hooks, bell. (1995). "Whiteness in the Black imagination." In *Killing Rage: Ending Racism*. New York: Holt and Company, pp. 31–50.

Jung, C. G. (1961/1993). *Memories, Dreams, Reflections* (13th ed.). New York: Random House.

Kimbles, Samuel L. (2014). *Phantom Narratives: The Unseen Contributions of Culture to Psyche*. Lanham, MD: Rowman & Littlefield.

Kimbles, Samuel L. and Thomas Singer (eds.). (2004). *The Cultural Complex: Contemporary Jungian Perspectives on Psyche and Society*. New York: Brunner–Routledge.

Kovel, Joel. (1989). *White Racism: A Psychohistory*. London: Free Association Books.

Mckenzie-Mavinga, Isha. (2009). *Black Issues in the Therapeutic Process*. London: Palgrave Macmillan.

Morgan, Helen. (2008). "Issues of 'race' in psychoanalytic psychotherapy: Whose problem is it anyway?" *British Journal of Psychotherapy*, v. 24, issue 1, pp. 34–49.

Samuels, Andrew. (1993). *The Political Psyche*. London: Routledge.

Singer, Thomas (ed.). 2000. *The Vision Thing: Myth, Politics and Psyche in the World*. London: Routledge.

Young-Eisendrath, Polly. (1987). "The absence of Black Americans as Jungian analysts." *The Quadrant Journal*, v. 20, issue 2, pp. 41–53.

10
THE PROMISE OF DIVERSITY

The writing of this book has been about opening our thinking within the Jungian psychology community and within the broader field as to the issue of diversity. This is not diversity as in, "we have so much of it and this makes for a rich experience of exploring our professional and heartfelt work together." Unfortunately, it has been more of the lack of diversity and feeling the emptiness of this circumstance within the Jungian analytical community.

The unrealized or unconscious intention of Jungian psychology has actually been diversity since its very beginning. I understand this to mean not only because of the variety of information Jung sought from a multitude of sources, but also because the source from which depth psychology sprang was itself diverse and borrowed from that which is African. The search for something beyond the immediate ground one stands on is a part of our nature. We need and want to explore. This is a part of the beauty of being the human aspect of nature. As I have spoken about in previous chapters, Jung met the challenge of *making the unconscious conscious*. His willingness to search far and wide in service of the psyche is admirable. There is no question of his genius. I have shown by use of his own words and those of others in previous chapters where and how he was unable to be sufficiently inclusive in his model for all of those in the human collective. He was unable to put into practice what he was preaching.

Once again, in a paradoxical way, he was advocating for diversity, was himself an intellectually diverse thinker, but he failed to commit to the act of diversifying. His constructed psychological model for collective inclusion, when implemented, actually excluded millions of individuals because of their ancestry.

Perhaps, it is Jung's inability to have established a complete inclusivity—that is, of Africanist people—that causes the very noticeable lack of diversity today within Jungian circles. If Jung could have predicted how the tide was turning—in favor of an active multiculturalism, global elimination of colonial domination, the increase in cultural awareness—would his approach have been different? Would he have been willing to recant his racially negative psychological models with Africanist at the bottom or near-bottom?

When Jung died in 1961, the American civil rights movement had already begun but had not yet reached the heightened level it would achieve in a few short years by the time of the March on Washington in 1963.

The years immediately following Jung's death saw radical and vitally necessary changes in the social structure of American politics, laws, and government as regards racist policies. Amendments to the constitution and Jim Crow laws and the landmark ruling in *Brown v. Board of Education* predicted a racial future for America that signaled diversity. The rules of racial relations and racism were changing, pushed not only by African Americans following the modeling of peaceful resistance of Dr. Martin Luther King, but also by the fiery street style of the Black Panther Party, H. Rap Brown, and Huey Newton.

Students and political groups all over America were engaging the government regarding America's prejudicial involvement in Vietnam, civil rights, and women's rights. It was a time of radical social change and a decade of death and uprisings mirrored on the African continent, in Vietnam, and in the streets of America. The chains of slavery from colonial forces that had held African countries prisoners were being broken.

Jung did not live to see the transformation of what the world needed—accepting that those of African ancestry could no longer be held captive by false lies regarding low intelligence, the need for missionaries for "salvation," or the rightfulness of the theft of Africa's natural resources—think diamond mines. There was a promise of freedom everywhere and a lifting of consciousness; with it came the promise of diversity and all the benefits of human rights that segregation had denied Africans and the African diaspora.

A part of these human rights included the act of cleaning the slate, making a new beginning, healing old wounds. This has apparently not happened in terms of the relationship between those of Africanist descent and American Jungian psychology.

Jung left several former analysands behind who took up the practice and teaching of Jung's psychological models. Important related new ideas concerning individuation, the self, archetypes, the collective unconscious and more have gained increased recognition over the last 50-plus years since Jung has died. *Why has the issue regarding the lack of diversity in American Jungian psychology only been directly taken up by one American Jungian analyst?*

What is the fear regarding delving into this racially charged aspect of Jung's theoretical model, acknowledging the racism present in the "old" model and beginning to *image* diversity?

I understand that there might be a "sacredness" to Jung's work, his words, his ideas held by many within Jungian psychology. However, his basic theoretical model of the oppositional relationship, where there has to exist a *primitive, pre-cognitive group* below the more highly conscious White group, must be addressed and discarded.

This would be in service of raising our consciousness so that a true diversity can take place within the American Jungian psychology community. How else can it happen? Ignoring the problem of Jung's racist theories and language, as noted by Young-Eisendrath 30 years ago, Farhad Dalal 20 years ago, and Helen Morgan 10 year ago, is akin to ignoring voices in the wilderness, reminding us that the *problem* is still there.

Americans on the broad social landscape of consciousness have realized that racism does not just go away—it changes form, becomes more subtle. Sometimes it explodes because, as Jung has stated, we are energy and are part of a psychic energy field. *Something* has to happen with the energy of racism—it does take up space, consciousness, and conscious effort to invoke. Jung, because of his study of Africans, learned about rites of passage. How can American Jungians begin to take the language of transformation and change—such as rites of passage, initiation, and the rituals of becoming a member of the Jungian community—and begin using their voices and ideas to deepen Jung's theoretical models to make them more diverse?

One of the basic core values of American Jungian psychology is that it must have as its nature the *potentiality* for being different, for changing its own consciousness, for seeing into its own Shadow. The voices for change are calling even while a historical racial energy tries to remain silently hidden in the Shadow.

Included in *The Racial Imaginary: Writers on Race in the Life of the Mind*, edited by Claudia Rankine (2015), is the essay "Open Letter" by Beth Loffreda, in which she says the following. I think it is applicable to my discussion regarding the American Jungian Psychology collective silence as regards racism.

> I suppose what I am trying to say is that it is important, valuable, for white people to write about race. But not because it is brave. Let us reserve that term for more truly dangerous endeavors. Saying it is brave makes it special, optional, and somehow unchallengeable. When it could instead be remarkable, a matter of course. Not easy, mind you. Hard. But not brave. For many well-intentioned white people writing and talking about race is hard, but not in the way I want to mean this word. It is hard for us because there is the feeling, back there in your mind, that there might be a skeleton in the closet you don't know about, or one you don't remember.... What can I be accused of?
>
> It's there. Many white people react to that question with defensiveness or fear, which are both forms of avoiding the truth. Because there is a skeleton in the closet. There is something to be accused of. Because you are white. And you grew up in a racist country. And there was a moment, or many moments, maybe even whole decades of earlier life, when you didn't sufficiently transcend those conditions. You have been wrong.
>
> *(Loffreda, 2014, p. 210)*

Helen Morgan calls the avoidance of discussing racism and its effects among Jungian psychotherapists "cordial." The issue of diversity, racism within Jungian psychology, even racism within the broader field of American psychology all must be explored and discussed amongst those of us best able to have the dialogue.

Maybe, if there was more interest and involvement in promoting diversity, the American Jungian community would experience growth. I understand that being an analyst is a *calling*. I certainly understand the roots of this belief where the traditional healer first goes through the anguished suffering indicating a life of working with others in healing work.

There is a reason why members of the African diaspora, traditional healers from South Africa, Caribbean Blacks, remain outside the circle of Jungian psychology. Do we not wish to discover why this is so by engaging with one another in meaningful dialogue regarding how racism exists in Jungian psychology?

References

Loffreda, Beth. (2015). "Open letter." In Rankine, Claudia, Beth Loffreda, and Kap Max Cap (eds.), *The Racial Imaginary: Writers on Race in the Life of the Mind*. New York: Fence Books.

Morgan, Helen. (2008). "Issues of 'race' in psychoanalytic psychotherapy: Whose problem is it anyway?" *British Journal of Psychotherapy*, v. 24, issue 1, pp. 34–49.

11
SUMMARY
Healing through an Africanist perspective

I would like to conclude with a look at healing from an Africanist perspective. I remember hearing many times over the years since my initial involvement with Jungian psychology that it was for the privileged. It did not belong to ordinary individuals as they were either too poor, too lacking in intelligence, or too emotionally unavailable to enter into the necessary work Jungian analysis required. I think these are old assumptions still lurking in the Jungian collective Shadow that disinvites others from taking part in Jungian analysis and analytical training.

We make choices about how we want to be in the world. Jungian psychology has the ability to help us deepen our emotional and spiritual selves. This psychology can belong to us—all of us, who wish to share in its richness. The racism that exists in Jungian language, the silence regarding the racism that lives in Jungian training institutes, and the call for change must all be acknowledged.

I believe that the opportunity for personal and collective growth occurs because there is a willingness for change to happen regardless of the suffering one has to endure. The reality of life is that suffering will happen. This is true for everyone, but African Americans can have absolutely no doubt in this area. If we only looked to our history of slavery, we would know this for a fact.

When Jung ascertained that the dream image of Dreamer One was related to a Greek image of Ixion rather than, or in addition to, a cultural association for African Americans, this was the quintessential moment of recognition of the importance of the inclusion of a cultural consciousness in Jungian psychology. Perhaps this is the time we can move in that direction toward the light of this new consciousness.

Healing from an Africanist perspective: questions of discovery

I close this chapter with a review of questions in consideration of healing from an Africanist Jungian perspective:

1. What can an American analyst, trained in Jungian psychology to work with all Americans while honoring, envisioning, and being constantly renewed in his or her own cultural imagination, offer those seeking psychoanalytical work? This question is relevant for analyst as well as patient or client.
2. How does healing happen with a consciousness that must acknowledge that such a traumatic past that has existed and still shows itself in the on-going violence against African Americans? How can depth psychology—Jungian psychology—become a contributor to the collective American psychological healing?
3. How does the analyst make the invisible visible in the work—not negating the collective Shadow of racism while being aware of the analyst's own personal prejudices, hurts, and ego demands for the patient?
4. What are the analyst's professional responsibilities in the face of archetypal grief and the other energies that are generated by centuries-long African American trauma? How does Jungian psychology fully claim and embrace an American psychoanalysis so that it might incorporate into its vision a model of integrity for all, one that supports the healing of collective trauma?

Reference

Jung, C. G. (1977). *The Symbolic Life: Miscellaneous Writings* (*The Collected Works of C. G. Jung*, Vol. 18, par. 82). Princeton, NJ: Princeton University Press.

INDEX

Adams, Michael 109, 111
African American culture *see* Africanist traditions and African American culture
African archetypal primordial 49–61; amplification 60; Bantu rituals 57; "black magic" 60; colors of medicine 58; "cults of affliction" 51, 54; dreams 53–4; geographical research areas 54; herbal medicine 58; hospitalization 53; Jim Crow laws 53; lack of history, "sense" of 50; lexicon 56; lower state of consciousness 52; needing patients 52; nkita lineage 51, 54; "offended spirits" 56; "pollution" 58; "scholarly" ideas regarding African Americans 50; slavery, justification for 50; ukufa kwaban 57; umkhuhlane 57; Xhosa beliefs 53; Zulu culture 57
Africanist traditions and African American culture 31–47; African American dreamwork and cultural consciousness 37–40; children 45; conduit for healing power 33; countertransference experience 36; dream study 41; "dream travel" 37; Egyptian Mystery System 33; emotional healing 36; Esu 38; exchange of energies 35; feminine imagery 40–3; "good energy" 40; Greek philosophy 34; individuation (skin as culture) 43–7; infection 46; mana personalities 33; opposites 43; parallel experiences 32; participation mystique 36; "river cults" 35; Shadow 47; skin color 43; sourness of skin 48; "sponge" remedy 43; symbols 43; transference 32–6; Yoruba, healing amongst 33
AIDS: epidemic (1980s) 19; outbreak (first), fearful years of 18
Altman, Neil 116–117
American racial complexes 24–30; Black Panther movement 26; ego 25; hate crime 26; Ku Klux Klan 26; Opposites 27; personal complexes 27; psychic disruption 25; "river cults" 35; Southern racial rules 29; "stuckness" 27
amplification 60
analytical psychology 5
animism 91
Anthony, Susan B. 103
anti-immigration bias 16
anti-Semitism 82, 113, 100
archetypal grief (African American women) *see* women (African American), archetypal grief of
archetypal primordial *see* African archetypal primordial
archetypes 5

Baba Adetunde 38–9, 42
Baldwin, James 99
Bantu rituals 57
bed warmer 68
Bernstein, Jerome 82
Black Lives Matter movement 13, 76
"black magic" 60
Blackmon, Douglas 16–17, 99

Black Panther movement 26
Black Panther Party 125
Boa, Fraser 5
Boas, Franz 15
Brewster, Fanny 50, 63, 80
Brown, H. Rap 125
Brown, Michael 8
Brown v. the Board of Education 125
Buhrman, M. Vera 50
Burgholzli Hospital 5, 94
Burrow, Trigant 6, 94–5
Bynum, Edward Bruce 118

Catholicism 74, 105
Chang, Ann Anlin 91
child loss *see* women (African American), archetypal grief of
Christian religion 97
class determination 103
Collected Works 5; collective unconscious, turning point of 94; complex theory 24; distressing experiences 29; Greek mythology 93; joke 19; mother archetype 66; objective psyche 97; racial infection 12; seeing the African American as an American 14; sex prejudices 18; Shadow archetype 88
collective unconscious 5; activities supporting thesis 6; awareness of 83; nonracial nature of 7
color blindness 119
colors of medicine 58
Cory, Hans 55
Cottenham, Green 16
countertransference 36, 117
creativity, shadow of 78
"cults of affliction" 51, 54
cultural consciousness (African American), Jungian collective and 107–22; bad Other 119; call and response 119; color blindness 119; countertransference 117; cultural Africanist assumption 111; dreamwork 37–40; fraudulence 122; "global village" 117; intelligence quotient 114; Jews, Jung's relationship with 113; Jungian and psychoanalytical writers on racism 112–22; language 107, 109, 113; "moralization of color terms" 112; potentiality for being different 126; psychic imagination 111; "psychodynamic notion of psyche" 114; racial typology 113; ritual cleanings 107; vaudeville era 121

Dalal, Farhad 82, 113–14, 126
disinhibited social engagement disorder (DSED) 69
diversity, promise of 124–7; calling 127; false lies 125; lack of diversity 124; making the unconscious conscious 124; paradox 124; promise of freedom 125; Vietnam 125
Douglass, Frederick 99
dream analysis 37
dreamers *see* Saint Elizabeth Hospital, dreamers of
"dream travel" 37
Du Bois, W. E. B. 1, 99

Eady, Cornelius 43, 107, 110
Ebonics 99
ego 25, 78
Egyptian Mystery System 33
Ellison, Ralph 24
Emancipation Proclamation 98
emotional healing 36
empirical studies 6
Equiano, Olaudah 65
Esu 38
ever-present anger 69
exchange of energies 35

FBI justifiable homicides database 8
Feagin, Joe R. 54
feminine imagery 40–3
Ferda, Erzulie 74
Fish, Jefferson 105
fraudulence 122
freedom, myth of *see* racial chains and the myth of freedom
Freud, Sigmund 6, 12, 93

Garner, Eric 8
Garrett, Henry 50
Gladwin, Harold Sterling 37
Gleason, Judith 77–8
"global village" 117
"good energy" 40
Gosling, John 112
Greek mythology 93
Greek philosophy 34
Green, Beverly 52, 79
grief, archetypal (African American women) *see* women (African American), archetypal grief of
Gump, Janice P. 101
Guthrie, Robert 50, 88–9

Hall, G. Stanley 6
Hall, R. 43
hate crime 26
healing: Africanist perspective on 128–9; emotional 36
Heidegger, Martin 107
herbal medicine 58
Herodotus 34
Herskovits, Melville 34–5, 99
Hewat, Matthew 56
Hillman, James 109–111
Hitler, Adolf 100
Holloway, K. 40, 75
hooks, bell 108, 109–11
Hull, R. F. C. 100
human bondage 67

individuation 43–7, 74
infection 46
intelligence quotient (IQ) 114
"intelligence" tests 100
Islamic State of Iraq and Syria (ISIS) 10
Ixion 93, 96, 128

Jackson, Leslie 52, 79
James, George G. M. 34
Janzen, John 51, 54
Jews, Jung's relationship with 113
Jim Crow laws 53, 110, 125
Judeo-Christian symbology 38
Jung's early America *see* racial relations and racism (Jung's early America)

Katrina storm (Louisiana) 64
Kemetic Egyptian civilization 118
Kimbles, Samuel 117
King, Martin Luther, Jr. 101, 125
Knights of Columbus 7
Kovel, Joel 115
Ku Klux Klan (KKK) 7, 26, 97

Laie, Botoli 55
language 107, 109, 113; *see also* cultural consciousness (African American), Jungian collective and
Lévy-Bruhl, L. 15, 35, 105

Malcolm X 101
mana personalities 33
Marable, Manning 102
March on Washington (1963) 125
Martin, Trayvon 8
Mavinga, Isha Mckenzie 118
Mbiti, John 33
McGuire, William 100

Mckenzie-Mavinga, Isha 36
Meier, C. A. 59
Meyers, C. S. 50
Mindell, Arnold 59–61
mirroring 65–6
Morgan, Helen 114–16, 126
Morrison, Toni 40, 111
mother archetype 66; *see also* women (African American), archetypal grief of
Mother of Sorrows 67–9, 74
myth of freedom *see* racial chains and the myth of freedom

Nazism 19, 113
Newton, Huey 125
Ngubane, Harriet 57, 59
nkita lineage 51, 54
Nobles, Wade 9

Obama, Barack 22
Office of Human Research Protection 19
Omari 55
Opposites 21, 27; duality of 28; expression of 89; "splitting" and 29
Orisha 77–8

Parham, Thomas 9
participation mystique 36
Perera, Sylvia 84
personal archetypal mother 77–9
personal complexes 27
physical prowess (Shadow project of) 89
post-Reconstruction Era 7
post-traumatic slave syndrome 69
post-traumatic stress syndrome 101
Pratt Mines 17
presidential election (2016) 28
Prince, Mary 70
Prosser, Inez Beverly 53
psychic imagination 111
puer-puella situation 39

racial chains and the myth of freedom 12–23; AIDS outbreak (first), fearful years of 18; anti-immigration bias 16; Opposites 21; "primitive" influences of African Americans 12; racial complex 14, 20; racial infection 12; self-esteem 13; sex prejudices 18; slavery 21; Tuskegee Syphilis Study 18; White American collective 22; White Other 21
racial complexes 14, 20; *see also* American racial complexes
racial identity 6

Index

racial infection 12
racial relations and racism (Jung's early America) 4–11; analytical psychology 5; archetypes 5; collective unconscious 5; cultural differences 10; dark characteristics 4; empirical studies 6; ironic situation 2; "permitted" violence 8; post-Reconstruction Era 7; primitive cultural foundation 2; race riot 7; racial identity 6; Shadow archetype 4; "testing" of African Americans 6; Underground Railroad 2
racial typology 113
racist socialization 69
Rankine, Claudia 126
Rashidi, Rinoco 37
reactive attachment disorder (RAD) 69
Reconstruction years 77
Republican Party's nominee (2016) 28
"river cults" 35
Robbins, Richard 104
Robinson, Jackie 90
Roof, Dylann 26
Russell, K. 43

Saint Elizabeth Hospital, dreamers of 93–105; African Americans and trauma 100–5; Catholicism 105; collective unconscious, turning point of 94; cultural consciousness 99; dreamer's individual consciousness 94; Ebonics 99; Greek mythology 93; "intelligence" tests 100; irony 102; post-traumatic stress syndrome 101; social stratification 103; Tavistock II lecture 95–6; torture 98; wars (American), Black men fighting in 102–3
Samuels, Andrew 113
Santeria practices 35
sex prejudices 18
Shadow (Jungian) 81–92; animism 91; anti-Semitism 82; archetype 4, 82, 88; carrying the Shadow 88–92; designated object of projection 83; dreaming the shadow 81–4; dream quality 85; legacy 91; opposites 89; personal dream 84–6; physical prowess (Shadow project of) 89; projections 81; slavery, immorality of 91; Tavistock Jungian group experience 87; theory perspectives 83; uncontrolled or scarcely controlled emotions 90; White Shadow 88
shadow of creativity 78
Sikes, Melvin P. 54
Singer, Thomas 117

slavery 21; as archetypal event 66–7; Civil War and 102; fragmented mirror 73–5; immorality of 91; justification for 50; plantation days of 121
Smith, Barbara Fletchman 116
Smith, Celestine 113
Smith, Susan 110
social stratification 103
Southern racial rules 29
Spradley, James 103, 105
Statistical Manual of Mental Disorders (DSM) 69, 77
Sumner, Francis Cecil 53

Tavistock II lecture 95–6
Till, Emmett 110
Tiso School 50
torture 98
trauma 100–5
Tulsa, Oklahoma race riot (1921) 7
Turner, Victor 15, 51
Tuskegee Syphilis Study 18

ukufa kwaban 57
umkhuhlane 57
Underground Railroad 2

vacant esteem 69
vaudeville era 121
Vietnam 125
Vodun practices 35
von Franz, Marie-Louise 5

Walker, Alice 40
Wall Street Crash of 1929 13
wars (American), Black men fighting in 102–3
White, Joseph L. 9
White, William Alanson 6, 7, 95
White American collective 22
White collective Shadow, projected idea of 90
White Other 21
White Shadow 88
Wilson, M. 43
women (African American), archetypal grief of 63–80; bed warmer 68; birth and naming rites 64; Black Lives Matter movement 13, 76; defining the archetypal 66; defining archetypal grief 67–9; ego strengthening 78; "flooding" by the unconscious 74; fragmented mirror (slavery) 73–5; human bondage 67; individuation 74; Jungian clinical picture 73–5; Katrina storm (Louisiana) 64; "metaphor" 74;

mirroring 65–6; mirror's poor repair (reconstruction and beyond) 76–80; mirror as a whole 63–5; Mother of Sorrows 67–9, 74; patient case narrative 69–73, 73–5; personal archetypal mother 77–9; post-traumatic slave syndrome 69; psychology of survival 76–7; Reconstruction years 77; shadow of creativity 78; slavery as archetypal event 66–7; sons 75–6
Wright, Richard 24

Xhosa beliefs 50, 53
Xion 6

Yoruba: healing amongst 33; sacred art form of 37
Young-Eisendrath, Polly 82, 112, 119, 126

Zeus 96
Zimmerman, George 8
Zulu culture 57